D1611949

A
DESCRIPTION
Of the ENGLISH PROVINCE of
CAROLANA,

By the *Spaniards* call'd

FLORIDA,

And by the *French*

La LOUISIANE.

Colonel Daniel Coxe, 1673–1739.

A

DESCRIPTION

Of the ENGLISH PROVINCE of

CAROLANA,

By the *Spaniards* call'd

FLORIDA,

And by the *French*

La LOUISIANE.

By DANIEL COXE, *Esq;*

A FACSIMILE REPRODUCTION
of the 1722 EDITION
with an INTRODUCTION
by *William S. Coker*
and an INDEX
by *Polly Coker.*

BICENTENNIAL FLORIDIANA
FACSIMILE SERIES.

A UNIVERSITY OF FLORIDA BOOK.

THE UNIVERSITY PRESSES OF FLORIDA.
GAINESVILLE 1976.

THE BICENTENNIAL FLORIDIANA
FACSIMILE SERIES
published under the sponsorship of the
BICENTENNIAL COMMISSION OF FLORIDA
SAMUEL PROCTOR, *General Editor.*

A FACSIMILE REPRODUCTION
OF THE 1722 EDITION
WITH PREFATORY MATERIAL, INTRODUCTION,
AND INDEX ADDED.

NEW MATERIAL COPYRIGHT © 1976
BY THE BOARD OF REGENTS
OF THE STATE OF FLORIDA.
All rights reserved.

PRINTED IN FLORIDA.

Library of Congress Cataloging in Publication Data

Coxe, Daniel, 1673–1739.

A description of the English province of Carolana, by the Spaniards call'd Florida, and by the French La Louisiane.

(Bicentennial Floridiana facsimile series)
Photo reprint of the 1722 ed. published by B. Crowse, London.
"A University of Florida book."
Includes bibliographical references and indexes.
1. Mississippi Valley—Description and travel. I. Title: A description of the English province of Carolana . . .
F352.C86 1976   917.7   76–18184
ISBN 0–8130–0402–0

BICENTENNIAL
COMMISSION
OF FLORIDA.

GENERAL EDITOR'S PREFACE.

HE post-Civil-War era made it a commonplace thing for railroad companies and promoters and developers like Hamilton Disston and Henry Morrison Flagler to advertise Florida. They were responsible for the publication of all kinds of printed material designed to sell land to prospective settlers. In the twentieth century, particularly during the boom era of the 1920s and the years since World War II, the promotion of Florida land has come to be recognized almost as a way of life. Large and small developers have printed and circulated books, pamphlets, articles, brochures, photographic essays, and a variety of other materials. The effort to

advertise and promote Florida to would-be settlers had its beginnings in the book published
in 1722 which is being reprinted as one of the
facsimiles in the Bicentennial Floridiana Facsimile Series. *A Description of the English Province
of Carolana, by the Spaniards call'd Florida, and
by the French, La Louisiane* was written by Colonel Daniel Coxe, who hoped to entice colonists
to the vast tract of land, Carolana, which the
family had acquired at the end of the seventeenth
century. It was quite a property, about one-
eighth the total land area of Canada and the
United States, and the largest grant by the English crown in America to a private individual.
Carolana extended from 31° to 36° north latitude, or from the River St. Mattheo (the St.
Johns River) north to Passo Magno (Albemarle
Sound) and west to the South-Sea. Dr. Daniel
Coxe, the colonel's father, developed the first
plans to establish the colony. Many of the con-
cepts which he devised for the governing of his
colony anticipated the later Oglethorpe settlement in Georgia.

At the very moment that Dr. Coxe was trying to develop Carolana, the French were de-
veloping their plans for colonizing the Gulf
Coast. The Spanish in Florida were particularly
alarmed at these threats to their security, although they took no steps until the enemy was
already approaching their threshold. They were
spurred to action early in 1698 when it was re-

ported that he French were fitting out four ships
for an expedition to the Gulf of Mexico. After
the years of procrastination and delay, the Spanish now moved rapidly, and a settlement was
made at Pensacola Bay on November 17, 1698.

Earlier that year, May 2, 1698, Dr. Coxe had
transferred 500,000 acres of land west of the
Apalachicola River to Sir William Waller and
his French Huguenot associates. The conditions
of the transfer required that the new owners
settle 200 Protestant families on the land in two
years. Shortly after this transaction, a one-page
pamphlet, *Proposals for Settling a Colony in
Florida*, appeared. Extolling the valuable products of Florida and the prospects for trade, Dr.
Coxe invited dispersed Protestants in England
and northern Europe to settle in Florida. There
was enough of a response for him to fill two
small brigantines which left England in October
1698 for the Gulf Coast. The Spanish arrived
in Pensacola in November, and a French expedition under Pierre Lemoyne, Sieur d'Iberville
settled at Biloxi, February 22, 1699.

Dr. Coxe and his associates were pushing
their settlement plans for Carolana. The brigantines arrived in Charleston where they were
forced to remain through the winter. The following spring, one vessel sailed south along the
Florida east coast, around the Keys, and into
the Gulf of Mexico, past both Pensacola and
Biloxi without observing the settlements. The

English ship explored the Mississippi, and there
encountered d'Iberville's brother, who had entered the river earlier. Although the English
claimed prior settlement rights, the French persuaded the captain of Coxe's expedition to with-
draw.

If Dr. Coxe had failed, he had helped precipi-
tate the French-Spanish settlement race for the
Gulf Coast. The War of the Spanish Secession,
which involved the great powers of Europe,
seriously interrupted Dr. Coxe's promotional
enterprises. His interest in America continued,
however, and he tried to keep the Carolana
project alive. More and more, though, it had
become the responsibility of his son, Daniel
Coxe, the author of *A Description of the English Province of Carolana, by the Spaniards
call'd Florida, and by the French, La Louisiane*.
The publication of this volume was intended to
revive interest in Carolana. In the preface, Coxe
explained that the purpose of his book was to
provide a description of the colony, the Indian
nations, and the flora and fauna of the area. It
was also designed to defend Britain's claim to
the province and to show what an attractive
place it would be for settlement. The project
was never successful. The Coxe family continued to hold title to it until 1769 when, finally,
Daniel Coxe V surrendered the claim in exchange for a crown grant of 100,000 acres in
New York.

If the book had value in the eighteenth century in focusing attention on an area about which so little was known, it continues to have value for twentieth-century scholars who are working in Florida and Southern history. It provides interesting data on the Indians and on the resources of the Carolana area. Many questions as to its accuracy have been raised, and there is good reason to doubt some of Dr. Coxe's statements. Yet as Professor Coker, the author of the introduction to the facsimile, notes, "Colonel Coxe's *Carolana* has earned its niche in the literature of the colonial history of America."

This facsimile is one of the twenty-five being published under the auspices of the Florida Bicentennial Commission as part of its program of Bicentennial activities. To plan Florida's role and involvement in the national celebration, the Florida legislature created the Commission in 1970. Governor Reubin O'D. Askew serves as its chairman. Other members represent the Florida legislature and several state agencies. Also, ten persons are appointed public members by the governor. Florida is the oldest state in the United States, and it is the fastest growing major state. All Floridians and all Americans are interested in knowing and sharing in its rich heritage. Publication of the facsimiles of the twenty-five rare, out-of-print volumes will make a substantial contribution to the scholarship of Florida history. The titles were selected to represent the whole spectrum of Florida's rich and exciting history. Scholars with a special interest and knowledge of Florida history will edit each volume, write an introduction, and compile an index.

William Coker, professor of history at the University of West Florida, is a graduate of the University of Southern Mississippi and the University of Oklahoma. The Spanish borderlands, Latin American and United States diplomatic history, and Florida history are his special research areas of interest. Professor Coker has been actively involved in the activities of the Gulf Coast History and Humanities Conference, and is the editor of *The Americanization of the Gulf Coast, 1803–1850*. He is editor of the Papers of Panton, Leslie and Company, and his articles have appeared in scholarly journals in the United States and Latin America.

SAMUEL PROCTOR.
General Editor of the
BICENTENNIAL FLORIDIANA
FACSIMILE SERIES.

University of Florida.

INTRODUCTION.

HE Rose and Crown press located in St. Paul's Churchyard, London, printed in 1722 a volume entitled *A Description of the English Province of Carolana, by the Spaniards call'd Florida, and by the French, La Louisiane.*[1] Published as promotional literature by Colonel Daniel Coxe to defend the family title to Carolana, to attract settlers to America, and to assert the priority of British claims to the Mississippi Valley, the volume has been the subject of praise or censure ever since. The book capped a half century of collection of travel accounts, maps, and writings about America by Coxe's father, Dr. Daniel Coxe.

The first Daniel Coxe of interest to this study, the colonel's grandfather, came from

Stoke Newington, now a borough of London. He died on September 3, 1686, and was buried in the church there. His son, Daniel Coxe II, born in 1640 or 1641, had lived to about age ninety when he died on January 19, 1730. Dr. Daniel Coxe II married Rebecca, daughter of John Coldham, an alderman of London, on May 12, 1671, and Daniel Coxe III, the colonel, was the first son of this union.

Dr. Coxe lived on Aldersgate Street in London for many years, but by 1723 he had moved to Hoxton. He had revealed an active interest in science before receiving his degree in medicine from Cambridge in 1669. He performed an experiment upon animals, using nicotine of tobacco, and had read a paper on that subject to the faculty of Gresham College on May 3, 1665. It was about the same time that the Royal Society elected Coxe to membership in that distinguished body. Two papers written by him appeared in the Philosophical Transactions of 1674: *A Discourse on Alcalizates and Fixed Salts*, *A Way of extracting Volatile Salt and Spirit out of Vegetables*, and *The Improvement of Cornwall by Sea Sand*. Coxe owned a chemical laboratory and once described the picturesque effects produced by crystallization during one of his experiments. He became physician to Charles II and later to Queen Anne. The Royal College of Physicians of London admitted Dr. Coxe as an Honorary Fellow on September 30,

1680. He was noted as a "physician of eminence, a man of learning, and an author."[2]

Besides his interests and writing about scientific and medical subjects, Dr. Coxe wrote the preface to *A Short Account of the Kingdoms around the Euxine and Caspian Seas*, which was published along with other works in 1677 by J. Phillip.[3] Dr. Coxe next turned his attention and literary talents to the New World. In this connection he has been characterized as a "man of grandiose ideas & one of the great American speculators of his age."[4] He was first interested in the Jerseys, and in 1684 acquired an interest in West Jersey. Two years later Coxe purchased property in East Jersey. On February 26, 1686, he bought from the heirs of Edward Byllinge an extensive estate and the right of government in West Jersey. Within a short time his land in the Jerseys and elsewhere in America exceeded one million acres. Coxe established the seat of government for West Jersey in Burlington, where his agents and deputy governor settled. John Skene, Byllinge's deputy, acted for Coxe until Skene's death in December 1687, after which Coxe appointed Edward Hunloke as deputy governor.[5]

Dr. Coxe and Governor Robert Barclay of East Jersey agreed upon a boundary line between the two colonies in 1688. This line was later challenged, but because of the opposition of Colonel Coxe, its resurvey was delayed until

1743.[6] Dr. Coxe sought to organize the Church
of England in West Jersey, a province heavily
populated by Quakers, and successfully solicited
the Reverend Thomas Bridges to move there
from Bermuda. Dr. Coxe's avowed intention to
bring the gospel to the Indians was probably
why he was proposed for membership in the
Society for the Propagation of the Gospel in
Foreign Parts.[7] Most noteworthy, however, was
Dr. Coxe's attempt to exploit his West Jersey
holdings, which brought forth his first piece of
New World promotional literature.

That advertising tract, published about 1688,
held out the prospect of great whaling and fish-
ing along the Jersey coast. There were adjacent
salt works, naval stores, and lumber of all kinds,
agricultural products including grapes for good
wine and brandy, mines and minerals, and the
possibility of a thriving trade with the West
Indies and Europe. Important to those interested
in early westward exploration and trade were
Dr. Coxe's assertions of significant discoveries
toward the Great Lakes. He claimed to have established a close friendship with the Indian chiefs
in that region where the French and English
trappers caught 100,000 beavers annually, and
he promised prospective colonists exclusive
rights to the fur trade.[8] The thrust of the article,
which he wrote from accounts of colonial travelers—Dr. Coxe never visited America and ac-
cepted somewhat naïvely such memoirs and

maps—was to advertise his Jersey lands in glowing terms.[9] With this tract Dr. Coxe had planted the seed which, nurtured by subsequent publications, would blossom full blown in 1722 in the volume to be published by his son.

In the fall of 1689 Coxe's Hall was built just above Cape May overlooking Delaware Bay. This estate, complete with quit rents and feudal services, is cited as one of the few attempts to establish a medieval manor in West Jersey.[10] According to Coxe, he invested £3,000 on whaling and sturgeon fisheries on the bay and sent French artisans to pan salt in order to ship salted fish to the West Indies, Spain, and Portugal.[11] An account in 1696 by Edward Randolph indicated that a Frenchman did pan some salt for Coxe, but the doctor's agent failed to pay the man, who went elsewhere and left the salt works to be ruined.[12]

In his report of the progress of his West Jersey plantations Dr. Coxe wrote that one ship of 30 to 40 tuns was under construction at Cape May and another ship of 130 tuns had been built either at Cape May or Burlington. At the latter place Coxe had erected a pottery at a cost of about £2,000 and claimed to have sold £1,200 worth of china from it in the neighboring colonies and in the West Indies where it was in great demand.[13] Dr. Coxe's enthusiasm seemed to inspire him more than it did his prospective tenants and clients.

In 1690 Dr. Coxe and others petitioned for
an extensive grant of land between 36°30′N and
46°30′N stretching westward from Virginia,
Pennsylvania, and New York to the South Sea
(the Pacific Ocean). This modest request included about one-fourth of the land in what is
now the United States and Canada. This was
part of Dr. Coxe's schemes for a vast inland
trading empire. The Lords of Trade declined
the petition.[14] At the same time, Dr. Coxe's Jersey properties were not doing well either.

The Andros interlude, 1688–1689, had
placed the Jerseys under the Dominion of New
England and its Governor Edmond Andros. No
sooner had that issue been resolved with the
flight of the king and the imprisonment of Andros, than war with France erupted. Coxe's an-
ticipation of attracting French settlers to his Jersey holdings, which seemed to have bulked large
in his settlement plans, were obviously dashed.
Even the prospect of the impeachment of the
proprietary charters threatened. As a result,
Coxe negotiated the sale of most of his Jersey
properties with the West Jersey Society, a group
of London merchants and businessmen, for
£9,000. He received £4,000 cash and took
a mortgage for £5,000. He reportedly made a
modest profit from the sale. By 1697, Coxe had
sold most of his land in West Jersey.[15]

During the years that Coxe worked to promote his New World holdings, he was also en-
gaged in commercial ventures in America. In

March 1687, he and others applied to the crown
for incorporation of a mining and trading company for New England. They planned to exploit
the lead and copper mines, forest products, salt
deposits, drugs, and dyestuffs of that region. In
the ensuing debates over the charter, the two
functions of mining and trading were separated.
King James II approved the petition for incorporation of the mining company, but formal
preparation of the charter was interrupted by
the revolution which deposed the king. Four
years passed before Coxe and his associates re-
newed their request. The new king, William III,
granted the charter for the mining company in
1692.[16] The problems arising from the French
victories and the lack of cooperation among the
various colonies during the last year of King
William's War, 1697, caused Dr. Coxe and
others on behalf of the New England agents to
recommend a modified plan of colonial union.
They called for New England and New York
to be united under one civil governor and suggested the Earl of Bellomont for the position.
The governor was also to have military command over Connecticut, the Jerseys, and the
adjacent charter colonies.[17] Dr. Coxe's association with the idea of colonial union is of interest
because it would later be more fully developed
by his son.

In August 1702, following the outbreak of
the War of the Spanish Succession, Coxe and his
friends petitioned Queen Anne to charter a com-

pany to deal in naval stores from America which they believed would be of great service to the crown during the war. Queen Anne granted the request in March 1704.[18] Nothing about the success or failure of these companies has been discovered.

Sometime after the disposal of his Jersey lands, Dr. Coxe embarked on a venture which guaranteed him a place in the annals of colonial America. Unsuccessful in 1690 in the effort to secure the vast area between 36°30′N and 46° 30′N, Coxe turned his attention farther south. Sometime between 1692 and 1698, the exact date is unknown, Dr. Coxe acquired title to Carolana. This province, named for Charles I, had been granted by that monarch to his attorney general, Sir Robert Heath, in 1629. Heath disposed of it to Lord Maltravers who passed it on to Coxe. The details of Dr. Coxe's acquisition remain a mystery. Carolana extended from 31°N to 36°N, or (as it was described) from the River St. Matthco to Passo Magno and west to the South Sea. It did not include the Spanish settlements of St. Augustine and New Mexico, but it did take in Norfolk County, Virginia.[19] Carolana and Carolina were two distinct provinces. Carolana joined Carolina at its western boundary.[20] The area involved was about one-half as large as that requested in the 1690 petition, about one-eighth the total land area of Canada and the United States. It was the largest grant by the

English crown in the New World to a private individual.

Geographic knowledge of America was neither accurate nor concise. Passo Magno is now Albermarle Sound and the 36th parallel passes through the sound. The mouth of the River St. Mattheo, present-day St. Johns River, was actually at 30°10′N. The point where the Satilla River empties into St. Andrew Sound, just south of Brunswick, Georgia, is almost exactly 31°N.[21] But Spain and England had not yet settled the Florida-Carolina boundary. The English, based on the Carolina grant of 1665, still claimed title to 29°N, a full degree south of St. Augustine. The contest over what is now Georgia would not be resolved for years.[22]

After acquiring Carolana, Dr. Coxe began to make plans to establish a colony on his huge grant. One of the early suggestions, the exact date of which is also unknown but prior to 1700, recommended the formation of a great commonwealth. Coxe delegated preparation of the charter and bylaws to a James Spooner, probably an attorney. They called their brain child the "New Empire" and specified that a governor, deputy-governor, and a dozen assistant officers should preside over it. Spooner recommended the appointment of several committees: religion, law, trade, accounts, poor, criminals, charity, and natives. Creation of the Imperial Company with a capital stock of £400,000 (80 thousand shares

at £5 each) was one of the central provisions of
the plan. Fourteen original proprietors were to
hold 20,000 shares, the rest would be distributed
among a thousand associates and others according to a scheme intended to entice subscribers.
In order to create a national interest, Spooner
thought that the associates should include some of
the outstanding public figures of England and
Wales. Two important features of the plan were
an obligation to bring the gospel to the Indians
and infidels and the transportation to the New
World of the poor, especially persons imprisoned for debts. Thus, they anticipated the Bray-
Oglethorpe project in Georgia by a generation.[23]
What Coxe did with the plan after Spooner delivered it to him is not known. There is no evidence that he ever presented it to the crown.
That Coxe intended to do something, however,
is amply documented. His ambition to plant a
settlement in Carolana triggered an international
contest which had as its ultimate objective the
control of the entire Mississippi Valley.

The narratives of two colonial travelers,
Father Louis Hennepin and Henri de Tonti,
inspired Dr. Coxe in his plans for Carolana. Hennepin knew of English designs to establish a
colony on the Mississippi before he wrote his
notorious *Nouvelle découverte d'un très grand
pays situé dans l'Amérique* in 1697, because he
referred to them in the book. He had even sent
his English correspondent (probably William

Blathwayt, a colonial expert and member of the Board of Trade) some information on the subject. Hennepin believed that once the boundaries of Carolina and Carolana were established, there would be plenty of room for both the English and the French. Dr. Coxe is thought to have been responsible for having the *Nouvelle découverte* and other travel tales published in London in October 1697. The London volume, *A New Discovery of a Vast Country in America*, ended with a bid for a colonization project for Carolana and referred to a map and an account of the natives, commodities, and materials of the region which was under preparation.[24] Likewise, Coxe secured a copy of Tonti's *Dernières découvertes* (Paris, 1697). According to Coxe, it was his copy which was translated into English and published in London in 1698. It is doubtful that Coxe needed any spurring for his Carolana project, but, if he did, the Hennepin and Tonti tales provided the inspiration.[25]

On May 2, 1698, Coxe transferred 500,000 acres of land west of the "Spiritu Santo" River (Apalachicola)[26] to Sir William Waller and several French Huguenot refugees, the Marquis Olivier de la Muce, and M. Charles de Sailly. Conditions of the quit-rent sale required that the new owners must settle 200 Protestant families on the land in two years. After seven years, provided all conditions had been met, they could secure an additional 500,000 acres of land.[27]

Not long after the land transaction, perhaps that summer, there appeared a one-page pamphlet entitled *Proposals for Settling a Colony in Florida*. It appealed for assistance for the dispersed Protestants in northern Europe and England. The valuable products of Florida, the prospects for trade, and other inducements were dangled before the public view. It proposed creation of two organizations: a company to handle all matters pertaining to land and trade, and a group of merchants to provide food and transportation. Sale of stock in the enterprise offered investors land and profits. A one-quarter share bought a settler one hundred acres of land, transportation, and food for the trip to the Florida colony. Meetings were scheduled at a tavern near Cheapside and at the home of the marquis.[28] But Coxe and his friends were not the only ones interested in a settlement in Florida (Carolana). France and Spain had been laying plans for expeditions to the Florida Gulf Coast for some years.

For more than a decade, the French had intended to follow up on the disastrous La Salle expedition. It was, of course, the same ill-fated La Salle adventure which had stimulated the Spaniards to renew their long-dormant plans for a base on the upper Gulf. Thus, on-again-off-again plans were afoot in France and Spain precisely at the same time that Coxe was readying his plans for an expedition for the Carolana colony.[29]

Coxe had seized the psychological moment.
Coxe's plans for his colony reached the French
Minister of Marine, the Comte de Pontchartrain,
in June 1698.[30] The following month the minister learned that Hennepin had been in correspondence with the English. France was not
worried about the Spanish pretensions to the
Mississippi Valley, but Coxe was a problem.
France had sent a secret agent to keep watch on
the English company. The Sieur d'Iberville,
leader of the French expedition, who had previously been informed of the English activities
and was already rushing preparations for his departure, was urged to even greater efforts by
Pontchartrain.[31]

For her part, Spain had intended to establish
a post at Pensacola (La bahía de Santa María de
Galve) and a cédula to that effect was issued
on June 13, 1694, but lack of funds prevented
occupation of the site. When news reached Spain
of the French expedition, a new *cédula* dated
April 19, 1698, made the establishment of a settlement at Pensacola a matter of urgency.[32]

The Spaniards were also aware of England's
interest in the Gulf Coast. During the summer
of 1698 Francisco Romo de Uriza, an officer
from St. Augustine, visited Charleston. While
there he met several Indians and was startled to
learn that they were from Pensacola. The English governor, Joseph Blake, countered Romo's
claim that Pensacola belonged to Spain, and as-

serted that France and England no longer recognized the Spanish title to Pensacola Bay. Blake
told Romo that the two countries had agreed
that when one of them first occupied Pensacola,
the other would recognize that nation's claim to
it. Blake also informed Romo that he intended
to take Pensacola the following year anyway.
Romo's warning of England's intent was sent to
Havana, but by that time the Spaniards needed
no further prompting.[33]

By the fall of 1698, Coxe and the French
Huguenot leaders had joined hands in their plans
for a settlement in Carolana. Coxe proceeded
with plans to dispatch several ships, and the
Marquis de Muce and his accomplices selected
one Ceuhu to head the advance party of French
settlers.[34] Two small brigantines, one under the
command of Captain William Bond, left England in October 1698.[35] That same month,
Iberville departed for Santo Domingo and the
Gulf Coast, and Andrés de Arriola left Veracruz
for Pensacola. The race was on! Iberville hoped
to beat Coxe's ships, and Arriola hurried to pre-
cede the French to Florida. The Spaniards won
the race, reaching Pensacola in November 1698.
Iberville arrived at Pensacola the following January, but finding that site occupied, he pushed
on to the Biloxi area.[36] Interestingly, two scholarly studies of the Spanish race to beat France to
Pensacola failed to mention Coxe or his expedition.[37] Only the English seemed unconcerned

about reaching the Gulf Coast ahead of their rivals.

When Coxe's ships and its passengers, which included a party of English gentlemen along with the Frenchmen, arrived in Charleston for provisions to continue the voyage, they decided to winter there. The leaders learned of the western travels and explorations of the Carolinians, and made plans to rendezvous with several of the Chickasaw traders on the Mississippi in 1699. One of the ships remained at Charleston and the *Carolina Galley*, a British corvette of 12 guns which had replaced the other, sailed in May 1699 with Captain Bond in command.[38]

Bond coasted westward along the Florida coast. He missed the Espíritu Santo (Apalachicola) River. He also passed Spanish Pensacola and French Biloxi without observing those settlements, and reportedly sailed on to the Rio Pánuco (Tampico). Coxe later stated that Bond only went one hundred leagues west of the Mississippi, which would have left him far from Pánuco.[39] In either event, Bond doubled back to arrive at the mouth of the Mississippi on August 29, 1699. Bond was aided in his search for the great river by a map constructed by Dr. Coxe from Spanish sources and believed accurate within twenty leagues.[40] Unknown to Bond, Iberville had preceded him by nearly six months and had entered the Mississippi by way of the Gulf of Mexico on March 2, 1699.[41]

During the next several days Bond sailed up
the river and observed that while he could not
make headway in the middle of the stream, he
could run up the side of the river where the current was not so strong. Some details of this part
of the voyage are contained in a 1766 letter by
Phineas Lyman who had Bond's journal with
him while he wrote. Traditional accounts give
September 15, 1699, as the date Bond encountered the Sieur de Bienville, Iberville's brother,
about 23 leagues upriver. If Lyman's account
can be trusted, the meeting was probably on
September 5 or 6 rather than September 15.[42]
Bienville and his small party in two canoes were
sounding the river when to their surprise they
saw an ocean-going vessel approaching. During
the ensuing conference Bienville informed Bond
that the French had established a settlement on
the coast. Because he had not observed the Biloxi
colony, Bond did not believe Bienville and concluded that the Frenchmen had come downriver
from Canada to trade with the Indians. Bienville
also told him that the river was not the Mississippi, but had a communication with it higher
up. Bond was not deluded by this obvious attempt to confuse him as to his location. Bienville
advised Bond that he must turn around and re-
trace his route to the Gulf. Bond retorted that
the area had been discovered by the English fifty
years previously and that the English had a
stronger claim to it than the French. Bienville

must have been surprised when Bond showed him Coxe's map which he had used to reach his destination. Nevertheless, Bond did not press the issue and left with a warning that he would return with a larger force and that he intended to lay claim to the country. This meeting place has ever since been known as the English Turn. Iberville, who knew Bond from an earlier encounter on Hudson's Bay, later referred to the Englishman as *un estourdy peu capable*, best translated as "a scatter-brain of little efficiency."[43] The sight of the English ship gave sufficient fright to the French that by February of 1700 they had begun construction of Fort de Mississippi, more rarely called Fort de la Boulaye. Located about fifty miles from the mouth of the river, this short-lived fortification was intended to protect the Mississippi from further English encroachment.[44]

Captain Bond returned to England in February 1700, about fifteen months after he had departed for Carolana.[45] The companion ship which had remained in Charleston had already sailed for England, but it was wrecked and all hands were lost on the voyage.[46] When Coxe introduced Bond to the members of the Board of Trade in mid-February, the captain presented them several maps which he had drawn of the Gulf Coast and Dr. Coxe gave the Board a report on the health, fertility, and pleasantness of the country.[47] The French refugees who had failed to secure a home in Carolana under English protection petitioned Louis XIV to be permitted to settle in the Mississippi Valley under the French flag. The French monarch, who had no sympathy for the Protestants, "replied that he had not chased heretics out of his kingdom to create a republic for them in America."[48]

The significance of the expedition Coxe sent to Carolana was several-fold. Inspired by the Hennepin-Tonti narratives, it had precipitated the French-Spanish race for the Gulf Coast. The Bond-Bienville encounter was the first meeting between England and France in the lower Mississippi Valley.[49] Bond's journal laid the basis for Lyman's arguments many years later that sailing ships could reach settlements on the Ohio and other tributaries by sailing up the Mississippi, even against northerly winds, more easily than French reports suggested.[50] More important, Bond's voyage up the Mississippi and later the sight of his maps at Paris created a sensation and established Dr. Coxe "as the leading exponent of the English transappalachian movement."[51] That movement had at its heart destruction of the French-Indian commerce in the Mississippi Valley and warned of the danger of French encirclement of the English Atlantic colonies. The meeting of Bond's corvette and Bienville's canoes touched off the contest for control of the Mississippi Valley which lasted until the end of the

Seven Years' War in 1763.[52] Before Captain
Bond and his French charges returned to England, Dr. Coxe seemed to despair for the success
of his little expedition.

During the winter of 1699–1700 Coxe sponsored several alternative proposals. On November 13, 1699, he submitted a memorial for the
incorporation of a trading and colonizing company. Coxe claimed to have determined at great
expense that the soil and natural products of
Carolana were ideally suited for settlement and
trade. He offered to surrender his title to that
province provided a joint stock company could
be organized and £50,000 raised by June 24,
1700. He suggested that the company be incorporated as the Florida Company, and that it
be granted the same privileges and protection as
other English trading companies. He requested
a large land grant to be added to the north of
Carolana. Aware that the southern boundary of
Carolana at 31°N did not reach the Gulf, he
asked for some small tracts on the coast to provide access to his lands in the interior.[53] Since
there was some question about crown jurisdic-
tion over the territory, Coxe followed his memorial with an interesting paper entitled "A
demonstration of the just pretensions of the
King of England to the Province of Carolana
alias Florida."[54] This assertion of English priority
in the Mississippi Valley, along with other ma-

terials which Dr. Coxe collected over a period of many years, served as the basis for his son's 1722 essay.

Although the attorney general upheld the validity of Coxe's title to Carolana, some adjacent islands, and Norfolk County, Virginia, the Board of Trade did not support his bid for incorporation of the Florida Company. The Board feared that a settlement in Carolana would weaken the crown's other possessions in America. If the conditions were as good as Coxe claimed, the Board held, the new colony might attract settlers from the older colonies and depopulate them. The Board had other objections as well. French Huguenots in Carolana might incite an attack upon them because of their religion. The Board probably recalled the Spanish massacre of the French Protestants in East Florida in 1565. The Spaniards were also certain not to like the idea of a foreign colony in Carolana for the potential threat it would pose to Spanish shipping in the Gulf. Accordingly, the Spaniards might retaliate against English commerce. In addition, there was the prospect that the colonists would engage in illicit trade and that the coast settlements might offer a haven for pirates. There was also the possibility of stockjobbing in the proposed company.

Still, the Board recognized that considerations of state were involved in Coxe's proposal and submitted it with their objections to the king

for his consideration.[55] Colonel Coxe later wrote
that this Carolana project met with crown approval and that William III promised to aid the
venture. Lord Lonsdale, Lord Privy Seal, and
other gentlemen also pledged their patronage.
Again, according to Colonel Coxe, Lord Lonsdale's death in the summer of 1700, followed
by the king's death and the War of the Spanish
Succession, both in 1702, forced abandonment
of the project.[56]

There is reason to doubt the accuracy of
Colonel Coxe's claims of such impressive support
for the project. On January 2, 1700, just twelve
days after the Board had listed its objections to
the scheme, Dr. Coxe proposed abandoning efforts to settle Carolana by way of the Gulf of
Mexico, and intimated that he would ask for a
grant of land at the head of the Morisco River
in Virginia, where he hoped to plant a settlement of those who had wanted to go to Carolana.[57] It does not seem likely that Dr. Coxe
would have offered to give up the Carolana project at such an early date if he had been promised
the kind of official support later implied by his
son. In fact, a Monsieur Galdie on January 25,
1700, predicted that the Carolana project was
not likely to succeed because of a shortage of
money and the opposition of the French and
Spanish. Galdie revealed that the Board had considered diverting the Protestants to Jamaica, but
because the French were not naturalized subjects

they could not own land and they did not have
the necessary capital for the development of
plantations on that island.[58] By that date, Dr.
Coxe had withdrawn his proposal of January 2,
and had substituted other plans, including a proposal to shift the French settlers from Carolana
to Norfolk County.

By January 8 Dr. Coxe had informed the
French refugee leaders of the difficulties which
he anticipated in establishing a colony in Carolana. Since he did not know of Bond's fate, his
fears at this point were undoubtedly motivated
by news of the French on the Mississippi. The
objections of the Board probably influenced him
too. At the time, the French leaders unanimously
rejected Coxe's offer to provide an alternate site
in Norfolk County and accused him of having
deceived them. They feared that they would
lose their investment and that they would be
taken advantage of by those already established
in Norfolk County. Coxe, who valued his reputation, argued that, on the contrary, he had not
deluded them. The controversy so upset Coxe
that he announced plans to publish an account
of what he had done in the New World during
the last twenty years which had cost him per-
sonally more than £10,000. If this account did
not reveal that he had always acted in the best
interests of his country without regard to his
own private welfare, he would be willing to be
censured.[59] If Coxe ever published the paper in

his defense, no copy of it has been discovered by this author.

A month later, February 1700, Coxe's plans were still not firm. He submitted to the Board a request to settle the French in either of two locations: at the head of the River Mattheo (the St. Johns) which he believed was in the northeast coast of the Gulf of Mexico, or, as formerly proposed, in Norfolk County.[60]

A few days later Sailly attended a meeting of the Board as a substitute for Dr. Coxe, who was ill. The Board was informed that Coxe, who looked upon the French Catholics as dangerous neighbors, still planned to prevent them from settling on the Mississippi. Nevertheless, he would await word from the Board about where the French Huguenot refugees should go. The Board also learned that the Archbishop of Canterbury had offered to provide charity money for the refugees on their voyage.[61]

A memorial from the French leaders on February 20 reported that they had negotiated with Dr. Coxe for a tract of land on the Nansemond River in the vicinity of the Dismal Swamp in Norfolk County. Because some of them were poor and distressed, they asked the king to recommend them to the governor of Virginia and to grant some assistance for their trip.[62] By March 7 the decision to send the French to Norfolk County was firm and the Board asked the king to consider the French request for assistance and to appoint them denizens (subjects) of England, which would permit them to enjoy many privileges not ordinarily accorded foreigners. On the same day, the king approved the request, designated certain forms of assistance to be given to the refugees, and authorized letters of denization for those petitioners that were properly certified before they left England. The king addressed a letter to the governor of Virginia, Francis Nicholson, and directed him to give all possible aid and encouragement to these poor colonists destined for Norfolk Country.[63] The king advanced £3,000 through the Committee for the Distribution of the Royal Bounty for the passage of the Frenchmen to Virginia and directed that Dr. Coxe supervise the emigration.[64]

The first shipload of the refugees—110 men, 59 women, and 38 children—under the general supervision of the Marquis de la Muce and M. de Sailly departed England in mid-April aboard the *Mary-Anne*. After a passage of thirteen weeks they arrived at the mouth of the James River on July 23. But Norfolk County was not the promised land they had expected to find. Because of the poor soil, unhealthy climate, and a boundary dispute between Virginia and North Carolina involving Norfolk County, Governor Nicholson decided against settling them there. Instead, he selected Manikin Town in the Piedmont, about twenty miles above the falls of the

James River, as their future home. On July 31
the refugees left for the new location, where
good land was available for them.[65] A few weeks
later, Sailly wrote: "We are, thank God, in a
fine and beautiful country, where, after the first
difficulties, we shall live well and happily."[66]

Governor Nicholson and the French leaders
were critical of Dr. Coxe. Nicholson had some
acquaintanceship with Coxe and believed him
to be an honest gentleman and an able physician.
The governor was familiar with the poor success
of Coxe's Jersey venture, and thought the doctor
had given up such projects. But Coxe had ven-
tured forth on two more: Carolana and Norfolk
County. Nicholson was afraid that some people
had taken advantage of Coxe's good nature and
generosity, had told him of strange lands, and
had supplied him with maps. He wished that
Coxe would come to America to survey his great
holdings, which he believed would include so
much of the country that he would not care to
come again. In spite of the happy ending to the
Muce-Sailly expedition, those two French
worthies considered their association with Dr.
Coxe and his Norfolk County holdings a distinct failure.[67] Coxe might well have agreed with
them. He had sponsored three projects: West
Jersey, Carolana, and Norfolk County. Not one
had succeeded, but their failures did not diminish
his determination to sponsor a winner.

The War of the Spanish Succession (Queen Anne's War) between England on the one hand and Spain and France on the other seriously interrupted Dr. Coxe's promotional enterprises. That his interest in America continued during those years is evidenced by his continued collection of information and documents about the New World. One student of the period believed Dr. Coxe responsible for the printing of the 1705 alliance between South Carolina and the Creek Indians. This broadside entitled *The Humble Submission of Several Kings, Princes, Generals, etc., to the Crown of England* appeared in London in 1707. In it the Creeks pledged to rout the French and Spaniards and not to permit them to settle in their territories nor within reach of their arms.[68] Such an alliance would have received Coxe's blessings because the Creeks lived in Carolana, to which he still held the patent.

The aftermath of the war in Europe gave Dr. Coxe yet another opportunity to assert his claim to Carolana. During the peace negotiations at Utrecht, it was decided to leave for later discussion the boundaries of the French and English colonies of America. In 1718 the appearance of Guillaume Delisle's map, which restricted the English middle and southern colonies to the Appalachians, created concern regarding French western claims. The next year Colonel Martin Bladen, a member of the Board of Trade, was one of the commissioners selected to treat with the French for a settlement of the colonial boundaries between the two countries. The Board was asked to draft Bladen's instructions, and the search began to secure all possible evidence to bolster England's claims to the American West. The Board summoned Dr. Coxe immediately. He jumped at the opportunity, hoping of course to revive his project for a colony on the Mississippi.[69]

Coxe produced his considerable collection of papers, journals, and maps, and a revised copy of his 1699 memorial at several appearances before the Board during the summer of 1719.[70] One of the most striking features of the 1719 memorial was Coxe's suggestion to draw the boundary with France at the Mississippi.[71] This meant that he was willing to give up his claims to Carolana west of the Mississippi for an unquestioned right to the area east of the river. After the conferences with Dr. Coxe the Board thought it advisable to get the settlement of Carolana underway at once. In spite of the Board's decision, nothing was accomplished, however. War between France and Spain in 1719, which saw Pensacola fall to the French, may have discouraged Coxe, but he did not give up his efforts to keep the Carolana project alive. In 1720 Dr. Coxe was suspected of trying to resurrect the project in order to make a bubble out of it.[72] But that attempt fell through, too. As for Carolana after 1720, Colonel Coxe picked up where his

father had left off, although Dr. Coxe lived on
for another ten years. Likely he played a significant role in the younger Coxe's plans to promote the colony.

As for evidence of certain English explorations and priority in the Mississippi Valley for
use at the Paris conference by Colonel Bladen,
Dr. Coxe could not find the papers necessary to
support some of his statements. His failure to
locate the missing documents undoubtedly caused
some of his contemporaries to believe "that his
numerous explorers' tales were indications of a
credulous temperament and a penchant for exag-
gerated statements."[73] Nevertheless, one of Dr.
Coxe's defenders has analyzed the 1719 memorial and has shown that only two of the five exploration tales related therein are questionable,
and even those may have some basis in fact yet
undiscovered. The two stories represented only
a very small fraction of the entire memorial.[74]

What does an evaluation of Dr. Coxe's activities to 1720 indicate? Presumably, he was a
good medical doctor, confirmed by his appointment as physician to two English monarchs and
by his membership in several prestigious pro-
fessional societies. As an author his writings cov-
ered medicine, travel, and promotion. No controversy has been disclosed over his medical
tracts. His travel and promotional publications,
which have undergone considerable criticism,
were largely incorporated in the 1722 publica-

tion of his son. He was a collector of New World literature, reports, maps, and related materials, although he was not always discerning about their authenticity. He failed as a promoter of colonial projects. Factors such as the three major wars between 1689 and 1720 diminished his prospects for success. Even without Coxe, France and Spain would have eventually occupied the upper Gulf Coast, but he served as the spur which hurried these operations. Several ideas came from Dr. Coxe's plans for the New World. The transportation and settlement of imprisoned debtors was original. He foresaw the desirability of colonial union when he endorsed the 1697 plan of the New England agents. He was foremost in his era as a propagandist for western expansion. Dr. Coxe was the first in England to promote the idea that the destiny of England in America demanded expansion west of the Appalachians. He warned of the dangers of French encirclement through their occupation and control of the Mississippi Valley. Contrary to his own personal interests, Dr. Coxe first proposed division of the continent at the Mississippi River.[75] Unfortunately, Dr. Coxe was a prophet crying in the wilderness. Colonel Coxe soon added his voice to that of his father.

Daniel Coxe was born in 1673, and was baptized in the church of Botolph, Aldersgate, London, on August 31. There are no details of his

early years or education in England. He probably
arrived in America with Lord Cornbury in 1702.
Subsequently, Coxe held a number of offices in
the government of the Jerseys. He eloped with
Sarah Eckley, the pretty daughter of John Eckley, a wealthy Quaker of Philadelphia. The
Reverend John Sharp, Lord Cornbury's chaplain,
who just happened to be present on the Jersey
side very early on the morning of May 8, 1707,
married the couple by firelight. Reverend Sharp
later christened the young bride. After a long
and stormy career in Jersey affairs, Daniel Coxe
III died on April 25, 1739, and was buried at St.
Mary's Church, Burlington.[76]

The first evidence of Colonel Coxe's interest
in America came in 1701, the year before he
emigrated. By that date the proprietors were
negotiating to surrender to the crown their right
of government in the Jerseys. That summer Coxe
supported the continuation of Colonel Andrew
Hamilton as governor of New Jersey, but by
December he had changed his mind and with
others presented a list of objections against
Hamilton.[77] Queen Anne ended the matter in
April 1702 when she appointed her cousin, Edward Hyde, Lord Cornbury, the first royal governor of New Jersey.[78] The following August,
Daniel Finch, Earl of Nottingham, recommended
Coxe as a member of the Council for New Jersey. In order that there should be sufficient va-
cancies, it was further recommended that certain

Quakers should be expelled from the council and Coxe and others appointed in their place. The Board of Trade advised Nottingham that all members of the council had good estates, but it was unaware that Coxe held property in the Jerseys. If that was not enough, the Board had already received twelve names for the council unanimously approved by the proprietors, and the group agreed that it should stick to those nominees.[79]

The exact time that Coxe arrived in America is not known, but his first stay was short. Perhaps he came with Lord Cornbury in 1702.[80] But whether he did or not, Cornbury favored him, and soon after they arrived Coxe was appointed colonel and commander of the military forces of West Jersey.[81] Little is known about his role in the military, but thereafter he was referred to as Colonel Coxe. By December 1703 Coxe was back in London, where he delivered some papers from Cornbury to the Board of Trade.[82] He had returned to England, however, primarily to defend himself against charges brought by the proprietors.[83]

The proprietors had advised the Board of Trade that Coxe had been recommended for membership on the Council of New Jersey without their approval. They stated that Coxe had no lands in New Jersey except those he claimed to have received from his father. The proprietors claimed that Dr. Coxe had sold all of his lands to them. They planned to proceed against both father and son in the courts, and to place Coxe on the council might prejudice their case. They also protested that Colonel Coxe had stirred up the people in the Jerseys by arguing that landownership should not be a qualification for election to the assembly.[84]

In February 1704 Colonel Coxe answered the charges against him, utilizing a tone that has been characterized as far more dignified than the criticisms lodged against him. He had been recommended for appointment, he claimed, without his knowledge, but he was willing that someone else be given the position. He denied that his father had sold all his land in the Jerseys; he still owned several large tracts there.[85] One study shows that Dr. Coxe conveyed 4,500 acres plus other interests to his son on July 29, 1701, who then disposed of this conveyance to William Penn on April 21, 1707.[86] Colonel Coxe contended that he did own land in West Jersey. During the ensuing years, he acquired thousands of acres in the Jerseys.[87]

While Colonel Coxe remained in England, Lord Cornbury was having problems with the Quakers, and he sought Coxe's aid in the effort to reduce the Quaker influence particularly in West Jersey where they were especially numerous. Cornbury recommended Coxe for membership on the Council of New Jersey.[88] The Board of Trade endorsed this recommendation, and

Queen Anne appointed Coxe November 29, 1705.[89] In the meanwhile, Coxe launched a strong protest against the Quakers to the Board of Trade. Coxe's opposition stemmed from his appointment to command the West Jersey military and from his near-fanatic support of the Anglican Church. The Quaker members of the assembly and council, he wrote, could not be expected to support the militia or the revenue bills to finance it since they opposed military service. They had also refused to pay tithes on pretense of conscience and opposed acts favoring the Church of England. The Quakers, he argued, intimidated and frightened those who might otherwise come over to the Christian Church. He asked the Board of Trade to prohibit the admission of Quakers to public office in the Jerseys since there were enough good people to fill the position without them.[90] He was unsuccessful on that score, and Colonel Coxe's animosity toward the Quakers continued over the years. A few years later he vehemently protested that the continued admission of Quakers to public offices hurt the Anglican Church; they intended to "destroy our religion, lives, liberties, reputations and estates."[91]

By the summer of 1706 Coxe had returned to New Jersey and had taken his council seat.[92] He quickly became a member of the inner circle, known as the Cornbury Ring. He led the anti-Quaker faction, and along with his co-conspira-

tors helped himself to the proprietors' lands.[93]
In 1708, when the opposition attacked Cornbury and his corrupt administration, Coxe defended the governor and blamed his problems on
the Scotch-Quaker-dominated assembly.[94] John
Lovelace replaced Cornbury as governor in December 1708, but the proprietors' efforts to prevent Coxe's reappointment to the council were
unsuccessful.[95] Although their protests temporar-
ily went unheeded, the proprietors continued to
complain about Coxe's position on the council.[96]
Conditions did not improve during the Lovelace governorship nor during that of his successor, Richard Ingoldsby, whose rule ended in the
spring of 1710.[97]

During at least part of the time that Coxe
served on the council, he was also an associate
justice of the supreme court of the province.
Cornbury may have appointed Coxe to the
court, but the first documented record of his
service on the bench does not appear until 1709.[98]
There is nothing to substantiate one author's
statement that Colonel Coxe "was an eminent
lawyer."[99] His judgeship ended about 1713, but
he returned in later years to the bench.

Robert Hunter, who became governor in
June 1710, proved more than a match for Colonel Coxe and his associates. When Hunter first
arrived, Coxe made overtures to him, and despite
the proprietors' cries of alarm, Hunter seemed

pleased to have him on the council.[100] It wasn't long, however, before the governor began to defend the Quakers from the incessant attacks upon them and sided with the proprietors in their efforts to prevent the continued peculation of their lands. Coxe, whose opposition to the Quakers was well known, was still in dispute with the London proprietors over his Jersey lands. Thus, on both counts—the Quakers and the land—Coxe and his friends declared war on the governor.[101] It quickly became a struggle for political survival. Hunter complained to London that unless Coxe and his friends were removed from office, there was no hope for peace and quiet in New Jersey.[102] Coxe retaliated, and among other charges he accused the governor of soliciting his removal because Coxe was a member of the Church of England.[103] But the Queen sided with her governor and dismissed Coxe from the council on April 15, 1713.[104] The colonel, his father, and brother Samuel, aided by the Anglican minister, the Reverend John Talbot, then endeavored to prevent the renewal of Hunter's commission as governor.[105] But they were prominent Tories, and any political influence which the Coxe family may have had ended with the change in governments following the death of Queen Anne and the rise to power of the Whig party.[106] Although Governor Hunter had emerged victorious, Colonel Coxe refused to concede defeat. Unable to continue influential in New Jersey politics as a member of the council, Colonel Coxe turned to the assembly.

In 1714, much to Governor Hunter's chagrin, Coxe was elected to the assembly through the political support of the Swedish vote.[107] Before the next election and without any foundation, Coxe and his henchmen spread rumors that the governor was to be replaced. Apparently the fear that Coxe might be a favorite of the new governor, whoever that might be, produced a majority for Coxe's party in the spring election of 1715.[108] Hunter accused Coxe of using false suggestions and the rum bottle to secure his re-election and subsequent selection as speaker of the assembly. On the grounds that the voters had been deceived, Hunter dissolved the assembly, only to see Coxe re-elected and again chosen speaker on April 4, 1716. The governor then prorogued the assembly until May 7. Coxe and his friends refused to attend the May 7 meeting, and it was May 21 before Hunter managed to get a quorum. Coxe was again expelled and declared ineligible for re-election. But he was re-elected anyway, only to be expelled for the third time.[109] This time Coxe circulated a petition for Hunter's removal. When the governor learned of it, he ordered Coxe's arrest. The council and the assembly also charged Coxe with disturbing the peace and forming a combination against the government. Coxe fled to Pennsylvania and then to England.[110]

During the next two years, Colonel Coxe and his father did their utmost to get Hunter replaced as governor. The fight became so intense that rumors circulated that the colonel and his accomplices had even encouraged the governor's assassination. But, for all his efforts, Colonel Coxe did not succeed, and in February 1718 the Board of Trade wrote Governor Hunter that his troubles with Coxe were over.[111] The colonel remained in England for several additional years, during which time he assisted his father in efforts to revive the older Coxe's Carolana project.

In 1723 Colonel Coxe was back in New Jersey. Two years later he was a candidate for the assembly from Burlington and, true to form, was again involved in controversy. Governor William Burnet, Hunter's successor, accused the sheriff of Burlington of favoring Colonel Coxe against his Quaker opponent. The sheriff had moved the polling place to the edge of the county without the Quakers' consent and had kept the poll open for two weeks.[112] Whatever the outcome of that election—it is not recorded—Coxe demonstrated his sense of survival when he became a member of the Council of Proprietors of West Jersey in 1728.[113] In 1734 confidence had been sufficiently restored in Coxe to secure his appointment as third judge of the provincial supreme court; he held that position until his death in 1739.[114]

During his residence in West Jersey, Colonel Coxe became one of the largest landowners in that colony, but his claims often led to disputes with others. On one occasion Coxe was a defendant in a suit over some land at Hopewell. When he turned the property over to two other persons, they were attacked and seriously beaten by a dozen disguised men. The assailants chased the two men off the property and threatened to murder the colonel. If the colonel was intimidated by the threat, it did not affect his continued claim to the property, which was left to his heirs.[115]

Whereas Dr. Coxe wrote of his extensive commercial activities in America, there is no evidence of any comparable activity by Colonel Coxe. In 1725 he was part owner of an iron work. When that property was put up for sale in 1739, it also included a grist-mill.[116] Colonel Coxe's wealth, whatever that may have been, appears to have derived from his speculation in land. He may not have played an important role in the commercial history of the English colonies, but Colonel Coxe does deserve brief mention in the history of the Masonic Order in America.

Daniel Coxe III was a member of Lodge 8 on the roll of the Grand Lodge of England. On June 5, 1730, the Duke of Norfolk, Grand Master of that lodge, deputized Colonel Coxe as

Provincial Grand Master of New York, New Jersey, and Pennsylvania. Coxe visited the Grand Lodge of England on January 29, 1731, and on that occasion his health was drunk as the "Provincial Grand Master of 'North America.'" Extensive research by Masonic historians has failed to produce any record of Masonic activity by Colonel Coxe in America. It has been suggested that the lodge known to have existed in Philadelphia in 1732 may have been warranted through the provincial masonic authority of Colonel Coxe. The same source seems to believe that Benjamin Franklin was made a Mason under the deputation to Daniel Coxe. In both cases there is nothing more than inference to Colonel Coxe's part in these events. The colonel's priority of appointment as the first provincial grand master of Masons in America is the only fact we have regarding his part in the history of masonry in the New World.[117]

Colonel Coxe's animosity toward the Quakers has been registered, but he disliked the Roman Catholics even more. In 1715 he and his party in West Jersey encouraged the residents not to pay their taxes because the assessor was a Roman Catholic. The colonel considered it a betrayal to the crown and to all true Protestants for any Roman Catholic to hold an office of profit or trust. In 1716 when he refused to pay his taxes, his goods were seized and sold at public auction.[118] On the other hand, the colonel was a staunch defender and supporter of the Church of England. He was one of the first subscribers and incorporators of St. Mary's Church in Burlington. In 1723 the Reverend Mr. Talbot credited Coxe with doing his part in maintaining the Society house and property in Burlington. There is some question, however, about whether he gave 200 acres of his land for a glebe for a missionary at Hopewell. In his will, written in 1737, he devised 100 acres for the use of the church at Maidenhead. His son, John, deeded the ground in Trenton where St. Michael's Church now stands.[119] Although the family's support was not extraordinary, they did make some contribution toward the growth and progress of the Anglican Church in New Jersey.

Unlike his father, who left a well-marked trail of literature which stretched over a period of more than thirty years, Colonel Coxe did not exhibit much of a literary persistence. Over the years he penned or endorsed a number of petitions and memorials to the London Board of Trade, which more often than not took the form of polemics. No learned legal treatises or judicial opinions have survived, if, indeed, the colonel ever wrote any. He authored one short tract in defense of West Jersey's claim to the Island of Burlington in the Delaware River. It contained something of the social and economic importance of the island to the town of Burlington, but the piece was hardly more than a sketch.[120] But

his obvious lack of literary experience proved
no handicap for the production of Carolana.

The colonel got along reasonably well under
Governors Cornbury, Lovelace, and Ingoldsby,
although the London proprietors were out to
unseat him because of his clouded land titles.
Considerable controversy arose over the legal
and ethical manner by which Coxe and his accomplices in the Cornbury Ring engrossed thousands of acres of the proprietors' lands. The colonel found things extremely unfavorable during
Hunter's administration, and the governor managed to oust Coxe from the council, the supreme
court, and the assembly. The combined efforts
of the Coxe family and friends to depose Hunter
fell on barren ground. Little can be said in defense of the colonel's attitude toward the Quakers and Catholics, except that it was not uncom-
mon to discover religious partisans at that time.
As an Anglican he was a strong advocate and
supporter of the established church. Although
not completely devoid of controversy, conditions were far less difficult politically after Colonel Coxe returned to New Jersey in 1723 than
they had been prior to his departure for England
in 1716.[121] His deputation as the first provincial
grand master of North American Masons indicates that his character was above reproach as
far as his fellow brethern of the craft were con-
cerned. Of his second appearance on the provincial supreme court, one New Jersey historian

concluded that "his judicial duties appear to
have been discharged with ability and integ-
rity."[122] Whatever his political and religious successes and failures he is best remembered as the
compiler and author of the description of Carolana.

The volume published by Colonel Coxe in
1722 was intended to revive the Carolana project which, despite the favorable endorsement of
the Board of Trade in 1719, had still not mate-
rialized. As the colonel admitted, the book was
compiled largely from his father's collection of
Americana.[123] Verner W. Crane called it the
literary salvage of Dr. Coxe's memorials.[124] A
glance at the facsimile reprint will show that the
book consisted of a preface, text, appendix, and
map.

In the preface Colonel Coxe wrote that the
purpose of the volume was to provide a brief
description of the colony of Carolana, the Indian
nations, and the flora and fauna of the area. His
account, he claimed, would be more accurate
than anything yet published by the French.[125]
Of course, the book was also designed to defend
Britain's claim to the province and to make it
attractive to prospective colonists. He con-
demned the seizure and occupation of the province by France as an insult to the British crown
and people.[126] Coxe believed that, provided the
French were moved elsewhere, Spain would divide the country with Great Britain. He sug-

gested such a division at the Mississippi River,
with everything east of the river going to Britain, except St. Augustine.[127] It will be recalled
that in 1719 Dr. Coxe had recommended the
Mississippi as the boundary, but between France
and England, not between Spain and England.
Because of the lack of cooperation on matters
of defense among the British colonies in America, Colonel Coxe recommended a colonial plan
of union.[128] This draft is often cited as one of the
most important, if not *the* most important, features of the treatise because it was one of the
earliest printed plans of union for the American
colonies.[129] Although there is some similarity
between them, it is an exaggeration to allege, as
one Coxe partisan did, that Benjamin Franklin's
Albany Plan of Union of 1754 was little more
than a transcript of Coxe's plan.[130]

Parts two and three are the text and appendix. The text presents an attractive picture of
the Mississippi Valley and the region beyond it.
The appendix consists of three parts: an extract
of the charter granted by King Charles I to Sir
Robert Heath, the Board of Trade's acknowl-
edgment of Dr. Coxe's title to Carolana, and an
abridged copy of Dr. Coxe's 1699 memorial.[131]
The final part, the map, is similar in places to
the 1718 map of Delisle and was obviously
copied in part from that map.[132] Coxe acknowledged Delisle's map to be the best of America
recently published, but he called attention to the

limits assigned the English colonies on the map by this royal cartographer of France.[133] The editors of the 1840 edition, taking into account the primitive state of geographical knowledge at the time, called it a well-executed map of astonishing accuracy.[134]

On the surface *Carolana* seems to have enjoyed considerable success. Between 1722 and 1940 seven editions of the volume were published. Clarence W. Alvord refers to a 1705 edition, but a thorough investigation has failed to produce it.[135] From all evidence, it must be concluded that a volume that early never existed. The first edition appeared in 1722. George Watson Cole thought that it sold out and rather quickly went through several new editions.[136] On the contrary, everything except the title pages in the three succeeding editions of 1726, 1727, and 1741, were from the 1722 printing. Thus, it was not a success. It did not sell out for nineteen years despite periodic efforts to advertise the original as a new edition.[137] Of the 1726 reprinting there is nothing to say. But an examination of the 1727 issue shows that there were two different title-pages. Typographically they were nearly identical, but close examination reveals that they were the result of different type settings.[138] In 1741 *Carolana* appeared as a part of *A Collection of Voyages and Travels* printed by Oliver Payne. Included were "The dangerous voyage of Capt. Thomas James in his intended discovery of a northwest passage into the South

Sea (in 1731–1632)," "An Authentick and particular account of the taking of Carthagena by
the French in 1697 by Sieur Pointis," and Colonel Coxe's *Carolana*.[139]

After a lapse of almost a century, Churchill
and Harris published another edition in 1840.
In their "Preface to the American Edition" the
editors praised the book: it threw light on the
history of the aborigines; after comparing its
statistical data with other historical accounts,
the preface claimed that the Mississippi Valley
once teemed with Indians; *Carolana* could serve
as a textbook for the original uncorrupted Indian
names (they cited the Massourites—the Missouri
—and the Meschacebe—the Mississippi—as ex-
amples); and it showed the value and resources
of the country beyond that of gold and silver.
The products of the region could be used to
produce a favorable balance of trade; commercial nations such as England and Holland would
trade gold and silver for these products. The
volume predicted the rise of King Cotton and,
the editors pointed out, it was Tench Coxe, Colonel Coxe's grandson, who played such an important role in the development of America's
cotton industry. This praise of *Carolana* by
Churchill and Harris was motivated by their
desire to achieve a better sales record than the
earlier editions.

Two later editions appeared. In 1850 B. F.
French published the account without the preface and appendix as part 2 of the *Historical Col-*

lections of Louisiana. And in 1940 the Sutro
Branch of the California State Library issued a
mimeographed reprint (Occasional Papers No.
11) sponsored by the Works Progress Administration.[140] The facsimile copy of the 1722 edition which follows this introduction makes a
total of eight editions of *Carolana*.

Since its first appearance over 250 years ago,
Carolana has received attention from a wide
variety of readers. In 1756 James Maury intimated that it had spurred Colonel Joshua Fry
in his 1753 scheme of western exploration.[141]
The anonymous author of *An impartial enquiry
into the right of the French King to the territory
west of the great river Mississippi* . . . (1762)
acknowledged that he owed many of his facts
to some authentic materials collected by Dr.
Coxe. It is believed he was referring to Coxe's
Carolana.[142] Phineas Lyman wrote in 1766 that
Coxe's imperfect description of the South Seas,
which he must have obtained from others, should
not prejudice acceptance of those parts of his
book of which he had knowledge.[143] In London
in 1768 there appeared *The present state of the
British empire in Europe, America, Africa and
Asia.* Since Florida was a new acquisition of the
British Empire, more space was allotted to it
than to any of the other colonies. The author,
thought to have been J. Goldsmith, included
material on the Coxes' interest in Florida (Carolana).[144] *The History of North America* . . .

(1776) discussed British claims to Florida and devoted nineteen pages to the activities of the two Coxes.[145] It is of interest to note that Thomas Jefferson, whose concern for the West was well known, owned a copy of Coxe's *Carolana*.[146] In 1816 the *North American Review* called *Carolana* "a crude performance, drawn from various journals and voyages, to impress the publick with the great importance of the region described, and to make them jealous of its occupation by the French."[147] About Dr. Coxe's title to Carolana, the same author concluded, "Probably there is no other instance on record of any private individual pretending to such an extensive property."[148] Jared Sparks, distinguished early nineteenth-century editor and historian, was especially critical of Dr. Coxe's memorial appended to *Carolana*. Sparks could not find any supporting evidence for some of Dr. Coxe's expeditions, especially his tales of discoveries to the northwest. As a result, Sparks wrote "we are disposed to doubt all Dr. Coxe's statement relative to English travellers upon the Mississippi."[149] Since Sparks, many historians and bibliophiles writing about the early western explorations have seen fit to mention the volume. If for no other reason than the continued attention devoted to it, Colonel Coxe's *Carolana* has earned its niche in the literature of the colonial history of America.

On the other hand, if we judge the book on

whether it accomplished its primary objective to revive the Carolana project; it failed. The Coxe family continued to hold title to Carolana until 1769. In that year Daniel Coxe V and the other heirs surrendered their title to Carolana to the crown in exchange for a grant of 100,000 acres of land in New York. It was within this grant that Cox's Manor, Coxboro, and Carolana were established in honor of the family name and the province which Dr. Coxe and Colonel Coxe worked so diligently to colonize.[150]

WILLIAM S. COKER.

University of West Florida.

NOTES.

1. Hereinafter cited as *Carolana.*
2. G. D. Scull, "Biographical Notice of Doctor Daniel Coxe, of London," *Pennsylvania Magazine of History and Biography* 7 (1883): 317–18.
3. Ibid., p. 318.
4. John E. Pomfret, *Colonial New Jersey* (New York: Charles Scribner's Sons, 1973), p. 61.
5. Gabriel Thomas, *An Historical and Geographical Account of the Province and Country of Pensilvania, and of West-New-Jersey in America* . . . (London, 1698), also published in *Narratives of Early Pennsylvania, West New Jersey, and Delaware, 1630–1707,* ed. Albert Cook Myers (New York: Barnes & Noble, 1959), pp. 346–47; Justin Winsor, ed., *Narrative and Critical History of America* (New York: AMS Press, 1967), 3:442; Scull, "Coxe," pp. 324–25, 327; Pomfret, *Colonial N.J.,* pp. 46, 61–62.

6. Pomfret, *Colonial N.J.*, pp. 62–63, 94–95, 160; Scull, "Coxe," p. 325; Francis Bazley Lee, *New Jersey as a Colony and as a State: One of the Original Thirteen* (New York: Publishing Society of New Jersey, 1902), 1:168–69; *Journal of the Commissioners for Trade and Plantations from January 1722 to December 1728* (London: HM Stationery Office, 1928), pp. 440–42, 438–39.

7. "Notes and Queries," *Pennsylvania Magazine of History and Biography* 5 (1881): 114–16; Scull, "Coxe," p. 324; Justin Winsor, *The Struggle in America between England and France, 1697–1763* (Freeport, N.Y.: Books for Libraries Press, 1895), p. 46.

8. Scull, "Coxe," pp. 327–29.

9. Clarence Walworth Alvord and Lee Bidgood, *The First Explorations of the Trans-Allegheny region by the Virginians, 1650–1674* (Cleveland: Arthur H. Clark Co., 1912), p. 232n184. Although Dr. Coxe made plans to go to America and the Board of Trade drafted instructions for him to do so in 1693, he never made the voyage, *Calendar of State Papers, Colonial, America and West Indies*, 1693, no. 138, p. 36 (hereinafter cited as *CSPAWI*); Scull, "Coxe," p. 325.

10. Pomfret, *Colonial N.J.*, pp. 48, 62; Lee. *New Jersey*, 3:60.

11. Scull, "Coxe," p. 327; Pomfret, *Colonial N.J.*, p. 62; Thomas, *West Jersey*, p. 352.

12. *CSPAWI*, 1696, no. 108, p. 54.

13. Scull, "Coxe," pp. 328–29.

14. Verner W. Crane, *The Southern Frontier, 1670–1732* (Ann Arbor: University of Michigan Press, 1964), p. 50. The Lords of Trade became the Board of Trade in 1696 and will hereafter be referred to as the Board of Trade.

15. Pomfret, *Colonial N.J.*, p. 62; Lee, *New Jersey*, 1:167; Scull, "Coxe," p. 325. The date of sale varies from March 4, 1691 to March 4, 1693; see Scull. For much on Dr. Coxe and East and West Jersey see John E. Pomfret, *The Province of West New Jersey, 1609–1702: A History of the Origins of an American Colony* (Princeton: Princeton University Press, 1956); *The Province of East New Jersey, 1609–1702: The Rebellious Proprietary* (Princeton: Princeton University Press, 1962).

16. *CSPAWI*, 1692, no. 2, 467, pp. 701–2; W. L. Grant and James Munro, eds., *Acts of Privy Council of England, Colonial Series, 1680–1720* (London: HMS Office, 1910; reprint ed., Nendeln, Liechtenstein: Kraus Reprint, 1966), 2:107, 193–95.

17. *CSPAWI*, 1697, no. 620, p. 318; Scull, "Coxe," pp. 323–24; Justin Winsor reviewed the intercolonial congresses and plans of union but failed to mention this 1697 recommendation, *Narrative History*, 5:611.

18. *CSPAWI*, 1702, no. 282, p. 187; Grant and Munro, *Acts of the Privy Council, 1702–4*, 2: 196–98; Scull, "Coxe," p. 324.

19. Scull, "Coxe," p. 318; Winsor, *Struggle*, p. 46; Crane, *Southern Frontier*, pp. 50–51.

20. William P. Cumming, *The Southeast in Early Maps* (Chapel Hill: University of North Carolina Press, 1958), p. 25.

21. See any detailed atlas of the Atlantic coast.

22. Herbert Eugene Bolton and Mary Ross, *The Debatable Land: A Sketch of the Anglo-Spanish Contest for the Georgia Country* (New York: Russell & Russell, 1968), pp. 69–70, 108–10.

23. Crane, *Southern Frontier*, p. 58; Scull, "Coxe," pp. 323–24.

24. Louis Hennepin, *A New Discovery of a Vast Country in America*, ed. Reuben Gold Thwaites (Chicago: A. C. McClurg, 1903), 2:672–73; Crane, *Southern Frontier*, pp. 51–54, 56.

25. Crane, *Southern Frontier*, p. 54; Alvord, *First Explorations*, pp. 231–34.

26. Various rivers on the Gulf Coast have been identified as the *Espíritu Santo*, including the Mississippi River, but the reference here is definitely to the Apalachicola. See Crane, *Southern Frontier*, p. 55.

27. Scull, "Coxe," pp. 320–21; Crane, *Southern Frontier*, pp. 54–55. See also Charles W. Baird, *History of the Huguenot Emigration to America*, 2 vols. (New York: Dodd, Mead & Co., 1885; reprint ed. Baltimore: Regional Publishing Co., 1966), 2:88–90, 177.

28. Crane, *Southern Frontier*, p. 55.

29. William Edward Dunn, *Spanish and French Rivalry in the Gulf Region of the United States, 1678–1702* (Austin: University of Texas Press, 1917), pp. 146–47; Robert S. Weddle, *Wilderness Manhunt: The Spanish Search for La Salle* (Austin: University of Texas Press, 1973), pp. 232–40; Lawrence Carroll Ford, *The Triangular Struggle for Spanish Pensacola, 1689–1739* (Washington, D.C.: Catholic University of America Press, 1939), pp. 4–21.

30. Frank E. Melvin, "Dr. Daniel Coxe and Carolana," *Mississippi Valley Historical Review* 1 (1914–15): 261–62.

31. John C. Rule, "Jérôme Phélypeaux, Comte de Pontchartrain, and the Establishment of Louisiana, 1696–1715," in *Frenchmen and French Ways in the Mississippi Valley*, John Francis McDermott, ed. (Urbana: University of Illinois Press, 1969), pp. 189–90; Winsor, *Narrative History*, 5:13; Crane, *Southern Frontier*, p. 48.

32. Dunn, *Spanish and French Rivalry*, pp. 171–74; Ford, *Triangular Struggle*, pp. 21–24.

33. Ford, *Triangular Struggle*, p. 27.

34. *CSPAWI*, 1700, no. 56, p. 37.

35. J. B. Tyrrell, ed., *Documents Relating to the Early History of Hudson Bay* (Toronto: Champlain Society, 1931; reprint ed., New York: Greenwood Press, 1968), p. 400. From all evidence this is the same Bond who sailed for Dr. Coxe in 1698.

36. Crane, *Southern Frontier*, pp. 56–57; Alvord, *First Exploration*, pp. 246–47.

37. Dunn, *Spanish and French Rivalry*; Weddle, *Wilderness Manhunt*.

38. Crane, *Southern Frontier*, pp. 56–57; Alvord, *First Exploration*, pp. 246–48.

39. *CSPAWI*, 1700, no. 124, p. 69.

40. Crane, *Southern Frontier*, p. 57; Alvord, *First Exploration*, p. 244; Scull, "Coxe," p. 319.

41. Richebourg Gaillard McWilliams, "Iberville at the Birdfoot Subdelta: Final Discovery of the Mississippi River," in *Frenchmen and French Ways in the Mississippi Valley*, John Francis McDermott, ed. (Urbana: University of Illinois Press, 1969), pp. 127–40; Rule, "Pontchartrain," p. 190.

42. Clarence Walworth Alvord and Clarence Edwin Carter, eds., *The New Régime, 1765–1767* (Springfield: Illinois State Historical Library, 1916), pp. 402, 415–18.

43. Crane, *Southern Frontier*, p. 57; Marcel Giraud, *A History of French Louisiana* (Baton Rouge: Louisiana State University Press, 1953), 1:80; Winsor, *Struggle*, pp. 45–46; Winsor, *Narrative History*, 5:20; Alvord, *First Exploration*, pp. 233n184, 244. Bond's encounter with Bienville could not have been much of a surprise to Iberville, who wrote before he learned of the event that he knew the English were on the west coast of Florida; Iberville to Monsieur Touenart, La Rochelle, October 13, 1699, original in Pierre LeMoyne Iberville folder, Gunther Collection, Chicago Historical Society.

44. Giraud, *French Louisiana*, 1:39–41, esp. 40n29 on location of the fort; Rule, "Pontchartrain," p. 191.

45. *CSPAWI*, 1700, no. 124, p. 69.

46. Alvord, *First Exploration*, p. 247.

47. *CSPAWI*, 1700, no. 127, p. 70.

48. Winsor, *Narrative History*, 5:20.

49. Jared Sparks, "Early French Travellers in the West," *North American Review* 48 (1839): 102.

50. Alvord and Carter, *New Régime*, pp. 405–21.

51. Melvin, "Daniel Coxe," p. 261.

52. Sparks, "French Travellers," p. 102.

53. *CSPAWI*, 1699, no. 953, p. 517, no. 1082, pp. 578–80; Petition of Dr. Coxe, Nov. 13, 1699, SP 44/238: 363–65, Public Record Office, London.

54. *CSPAWI*, 1699, no. 967, pp. 522–26.

55. *CSPAWI*, 1699, no. 1082, pp. 578–80.

56. Coxe, *Carolana*, pp. iv–vi.

57. *CSPAWI*, 1700, no. 2, p. 1.

58. *CSPAWI*, 1700, no. 56, p. 37.

59. *CSPAWI*, 1700, no. 18, pp. 22–23, no. 20, p. 24.

60. *CSPAWI*, 1700, no. 124, p. 69.

61. *CSPAWI*, 1700, no. 127, p. 71, no. 132, p. 73; Baird, *Huguenot Emigration*, 2:179–80.

62. *CSPAWI*, 1700, no. 146, pp. 75–76; see Baird, *Huguenot Emigration*, 2:177–78, on the location in Norfolk County.

63. *CSPAWI*, 1700, nos. 199, 200, 201, p. 113; see also no. 263, p. 140, no. 306, p. 156.

64. *CSPAWI*, 1700, no. 739 XIII, pp. 501–2; Scull, "Coxe," p. 321; Baird, *Huguenot Emigraton*, 2:176, 179.

65. *CSPAWI*, 1700 no. 681, pp. 448–50, no. 681 XI, pp. 456–57, no. 704, pp. 472–73; Richard L. Morton, *Colonial Virginia* (Chapel Hill: University of North Carolina Press, 1960), 1:367–68; Scull, "Coxe," pp. 321–23; Baird, *Huguenot Emigration*, 2:176–77.

66. *CSPAWI*, 1700, no. 739 V, p. 498.

67. *CSPAWI*, 1700, no. 739, p. 497.

68. Crane, *Southern Frontier*, pp. 82–83.

69. Ibid., pp. 59, 224–25; *CSPAWI*, 1719, no. 323, p. 174.

70. *CSPAWI*, 1719, no. 349, p. 186; Alvord, *First Exploration*, pp. 231–49; see Melvin, "Daniel Coxe," pp. 257–62 for a critique of the copy of Coxe's 1719 memorial in Alvord, *First Exploration*, pp. 231–49.

71. Alvord, *First Exploration*, pp. 248–49.

72. Melvin, "Daniel Coxe," pp. 258–60; Crane, *Southern Frontier*, p. 226.

73. Melvin, "Daniel Coxe," p. 260.

74. Ibid., pp. 260–61.

75. Crane, *Southern Frontier*, pp. 50, 59–60.

76. Scull, "Coxe," p. 326; *Collections of the New Jersey Historical Society*, 9:82–83; Hamilton Schuyler, *History of St. Michael's Church, Trenton, 1703–1926* (Princeton: Princeton University Press, 1926), p. 339; Charles P. Keith, "Andrew Allen, *Pennsylvania Magazine of History and Biography* 10 (1886): 364.

77. *CSPAWI*, 1701, nos. 745i, 745ii, 745iii, pp. 420–22, no. 1083, p. 681.

78. Pomfret, *Colonial N.J.*, p. 87.

79. *CSPAWI*, 1702, nos. 806, 806i, p. 500, no. 834, p. 518, nos. 928, 928i, pp. 571–72, no. 932, pp. 574–75.

80. *Collections of the New Jersey Historical Society*, 9:82; Robert K. Turner, Jr., "Coxe's A Description of Carolana (1722–1741)," in *Studies in Bibliography*, Fredson Bowers, ed.

(Charlottesville: Bibliographical Society of the University of Virginia, 1957), 9:252.

81. New Jersey Archives, Series 1, 3:44.

82. *CSPAWI*, 1703, no. 1372, p. 867.

83. *Collections of the New Jersey Historical Society*, 9:82; *CSPAWI*, 1704, no. 48, p. 23.

84. *CSPAWI*, 1704, no. 48, p. 23; New Jersey Archives, Series 1, 3:35–38.

85. *Collections of the New Jersey Historical Society*, 9:82; *CSPAWI*, 1704, no. 92, p. 37; New Jersey Archives, Series 1, 3:42–47.

86. John Clement, "William Penn," *Pennsylvania Magazine of History and Biography* 5 (1881): 328.

87. Pomfret, *Colonial N.J.*, p. 137.

88. *CSPAWI*, 1705, no. 878, pp. 381–88, no. 1010, p. 477; New Jersey Archives, Series 1, 3:68–81.

89. *CSPAWI*, 1705, no. 1465, p. 709, no. 1482, p. 722, 1706, no. 80, p. 38; New Jersey Archives, Series 1, 3:115–16, 124–29; Grant and Munro, *Acts of Privy Council*, 2:818–19.

90. New Jersey Archives, Series 1, 3:82–85; *CSPAWI*, 1705, no. 1010, p. 477.

91. *CSPAWI*, 1711, no. 58, p. 53, no. 58i, pp. 53–54.

92. New Jersey Archives, Series 1, 3:132, 160.

93. Pomfret, *Colonial N.J.*, pp. 125–28.

94. *CSPAWI*, 1708, nos. 1329i and 1329ii, pp. 662–64; New Jersey Archives, Series 1, 3:287–90; Pomfret, *Colonial N.J.*, p. 133.

95. New Jersey Archives, Series 1, 3:300–302, 316–17; Pomfret, *Colonial N.J.*, p. 129.

96. *CSPAWI*, 1708, no. 1597, pp. 783–84, 1709, no. 876, pp. 534–35; New Jersey Archives, Series 1, 3:497–98.

97. Pomfret, *Colonial N.J.*, pp. 129–33.

98. *Collections of the New Jersey Historical Society*, 9:82; New Jersey Archives, Series 1, 3:459; Pomfret, *Colonial N.J.*, p. 129 refers to Coxe's appointment to the court as an associate justice in 1709. Coxe's first appearance on the Court of Quarter Sessions for Burlington County came on September 13, 1709. H. Clay Reed and George J. Miller, eds., *The Burlington Court Book: A Record of Quaker Jurisprudence in West New Jersey, 1680–1709* (Washington: American Historical Association, 1944), p. 338.

99. Joseph H. Hough, *Origin of Masonry in the State of New Jersey, and the entire Proceedings of the Grand Lodge, from its First Organization, A.L. 5786. Compiled from Authentic Sources* (Trenton, N.J.: Pub. by Joseph H. Hough, Murphy & Bechtel, Printers, 1870), p. x.

100. New Jersey Archives, Series 1, 4:324–25.

101. Pomfret, *Colonial N.J.*, pp. 125–38; *CSPAWI*, 1711, no. 8, p. 2, no. 156, p. 137, 1717, no. 674, p. 355; Winsor, *Narrative History*, 5:219; New Jersey Archives, Series 1, 4:325.

102. *CSPAWI*, 1711, no. 832, pp. 472–86, 1712, no. 65, p. 37, no. 249, pp. 188–89, no. 413, p. 282, 1715, no. 436, p. 193; New Jersey Archives, Series 1, 4:51–70, 149–50, 153.

103. *CSPAWI*, 1716, no. 138i, pp. 70–71; New Jersey Archives, Series 1, 4:242–46.

104. *CSPAWI*, 1713, no. 315, p. 168, no. 324, pp. 170–71; New Jersey Archives, Series 1, 3:35–36.

105. *CSPAWI*, 1715, no. 164, p. 69, no. 229, pp. 102–3, 1716, nos. 176 and 176i, p. 97, no. 195, pp. 105–6; New Jersey Archives, Series 1, 4:199; Pomfret, *Colonial N.J.*, p. 136.

106. *CSPAWI*, 1717, no. 674, p. 355; George Morgan Hills, "John Talbot, the First Bishop in North America," *Pennsylvania Magazine of History and Biography* 3 (1879): 41–42.

107. *CSPAWI*, 1715, no. 435, pp. 186–88; *Collections of the New Jersey Historical Society*, 9:83.

108. Pomfret, *Colonial N.J.*, p. 136.

109. *Collections of the New Jersey Historical Society*, 9:83; Richard S. Field, *The Provincial Courts of New Jersey, with Sketches of the Bench and Bar* (New York: Published for the Society, 1849) in *Collections of the New Jersey Historical Society*, 3:92–99; *CSPAWI*, 1716, no. 135, pp. 68–70, no. 176, p. 97; Pomfret, *Colonial N.J.*, pp. 137–38; Lee, *New Jersey*, 1:391.

110. *CSPAWI*, 1716, no. 192, pp. 104–5, no. 349, p. 183, nos. 392 and 392i, pp. 202–3; New Jersey Archives, Series 1, 4:258, 260–62, 266–67.

111. *CSPAWI*, 1717, no. 523, p. 284, no. 565, pp. 299–300, no. 588i, pp. 312–13, no. 690, pp. 363–64, no. 195, p. 103, 1718, no. 344, pp. 169–70, no. 373, pp. 182–83; New Jersey Archives, Series 1, 4:291–97, 262–64, 315.

112. *CSPAWI*, 1725, no. 788, pp. 468–69; Schuyler, *St. Michael's Church*, pp. 12–13, contains a letter from the Rev. John Talbot dated Sept. 20, 1723, which indicates Col. Coxe, had returned to New Jersey by that date.

113. New Jersey Archives, Series 1, 5:211–12.

114. Field, *Provincial Courts*, pp. 132, 137.

115. New Jersey Archives, Series 1, 11:400, 431–32, 439, 581.

116. Ibid., pp. 586–87.

117. Hough, *Masonry in New Jersey*, pp. vi–ix; Schuyler, *St. Michael's Church*, p. 361; Conrad Hahn, Executive Secretary, The Masonic Service Association of the U.S. to author, March 5, 1973.

118. New Jersey Archives, Series 1, 4:213–15, 230–33.

119. Schuyler, *St. Michael's Church*, pp. 12–13, 32–33, 65, 68.

120. *Journal of the Commissioners for Trade and Planta-tions*, Nov. 1718 to Dec. 1722, pp. 281–83, 293–95, 362–63; New Jersey Archives, Series 1, 5:38–43.

121. In 1735 Coxe got into a dispute over a debt he owed Lord Clinton, which resulted in an exposé of Coxe's affairs by Robert Hunter Morris; Beverly McAnear, "An American in London, 1735–36," *Pennsylvania Magazine of History and Biography* 64 (1940): 194–95, 360, 364.

122. Field, *Provincial Courts*, p. 137.

123. *Carolana*, pp. i–ii.

124. *Southern Frontier*, p. 226.

125. *Carolana*, pp. vii–viii.

126. Ibid., pp. xxi–xxii.

127. Ibid., p. xxxii.

128. Ibid., pp. xv–xx.

129. *The Celebrated Collection of Americana formed by the late Thomas Winthrop Streeter* (New York: Parke-Bernet Galleries, 1967), 2:846.

130. Field, *Provincial Courts*, pp. 136–37; the editor of the Franklin Papers never mentioned Coxe's plan in his detailed analysis of the origin of the Albany Plan of Union, Leonard W. Larabee, ed., *The Papers of Benjamin Franklin* (New Haven: Yale University Press, 1962), 5:374–87.

131. A comparison of the 1699 memorial and the copy printed by Col. Coxe shows much deleted and some few things added. See *CSPAWI*, 1699, no. 967, pp. 522–26.

132. This is especially true of the Florida peninsula in which the two maps are almost identical and both in error. Compare *Carte de la Louisiane et du Cours du Mississippi* by Delisle, 1718.

133. *Carolana*, p. xxxvii.

134. Daniel Coxe, *A Description of the English Province of Carolana* . . . (St. Louis: Churchill and Harris Printers, 1840), p. iv.

135. Alvord, *First Exploration*, pp. 234n, 254.

136. *A Catalogue of Books Relating to the Discovery and Early History of North and South America* (New York: Peter Smith, 1951), 4:1836.

137. Turner, "Coxe's Description," p. 253.

138. Ibid., p. 253n7.

139. Winsor, *Narrative History*, 5:69.

140. Turner, "Coxe's Description," p. 252n2.

141. Winsor, *Struggle*, pp. 216–17.

142. London: W. Nicoll, 1762; Thomas D. Clark, ed., *Travels in the Old South: A Bibliography* (Norman: University of Oklahoma Press, 1956), 1:230.

143. Alvord and Carter, *New Régime*, p. 409.

144. London: W. Griffin, J. Johnson, W. Nicoll, and Rich-

ardson and Urquhart, 1768; Clark, *Old South*, 1:217-18.

145. London: Sold by Millar, etc., 1776; Clark, *Old South*, 1:225–26.

146. E. Millicent Sowerby, comp., *Catalogue of the Library of Thomas Jefferson* (Washington: Library of Congress, 1955), 4:207–8.

147. *The North American Review and Miscellaneous Journal* 4 (1815): 1.

148. Ibid., p. 2.

149. Sparks, "French Travellers," p. 104.

150. E. B. O'Callaghan, ed., *Documents Relative to the Colonial History of the State of New-York* . . . (Albany: Weed, Parsons & Co., Printers, 1855–56), 5:204, 7:926.

A

DESCRIPTION

Of the ENGLISH PROVINCE of

CAROLANA,

By the *Spaniards* call'd

FLORIDA,

And by the *French*

La LOUISIANE.

As also of the Great and Famous River

MESCHACEBE or MISSISIPI,

The Five vast Navigable Lakes of Fresh
Water, and the Parts Adjacent.

TOGETHER

With an Account of the Commodities of the
Growth and Production of the said Province.
And a PREFACE containing some Considerations on the Consequences of the *French*
making Settlements there.

By DANIEL COXE, *Esq*;

Non minor est Virtus quam quærere parta tueri.

LONDON;
Printed *for* B. COWSE, at the Rose *and* Crown in
St. Paul's Church-Yard. M DCC XXII.

THE
PREFACE.

THE ensuing Treatise is, for the most Part, compos'd out of Memoirs, which the present Proprietor of Carolana, my honour'd Father, had drawn from several English Journals and Itineraries taken by his own People, whom he had sent for Discovery of this most noble, pleasant and fertile Province and the Parts adjacent, both by Sea and Land; as well as from the Accounts of other Travellers and Indian Tra-

B   ders,

The PREFACE.

ders, *who had often pierc'd into and rang'd through the* Heart *of it,* and were Perſons *of* good Underſtanding and Probity, *whoſe* Relations *agreeing ſo well together, tho' moſtly* Strangers *to each other, it is not to be ſuppos'd, they could conſpire to impoſe* Fables and Falſities *on the* World.

THE *vaſt* Trouble and Expence (*thoſe* Two great Impediments *of* Publick Good) *the ſaid* Proprietor has *un-dergone to effect all this, will ſcarcely be credited ; for he not only, at his ſole* Charge, *for ſeveral* Years, *eſtabliſh'd and kept up a* Correſpondence *with the* Governors and Chief Indian Traders *in all the* Engliſh Colonies *on the Continent of* America, *imploy'd many* People *on* Diſcoveries *by Land to the* Weſt, North and South *of this vaſt* Extent of Ground, *but likewiſe in the* Year 1698. *he equipp'd and fitted out* Two Ships, *provided with above* Twenty great Guns, Sixteen Patereroes, *abundance of* Small Arms, Ammunition, Stores and Proviſions *of all Sorts, not only for the* Uſe *of thoſe on* Board, *and*

and for Discovery by Sea, *but also for building a* Fortification, *and settling a* Colony *by Land , there being in both* Vessels, *besides Sailors and Common Men,* above *Thirty* English *and* French *Volunteers, some* Noblemen, *and all* Gentlemen.

ONE *of these* Vessels *discover'd the* Mouths *of the* great *and* famous River Meschacebe, *or, as term'd by the* French, Missisippi, *enter'd and ascended it above* One Hundred Miles, *and had perfected a* Settlement *therein, if the* Captain *of the other Ship had done his* Duty *and not deserted them. They howsoever took* Possession *of this* Country *in the* King's Name, *and left, in several* Places, *the* Arms *of* Great-Britain *affix'd on* Boards *and* Trees *for a* Memorial *thereof.*

AND *here I cannot forbear taking* Notice, *that this was the first* Ship *that ever enter'd that* River *from the* Sea, *or that perfectly discover'd or describ'd it's several* Mouths, *in* Opposition *to the* Boasts *and* Falsities *of the* French,

who

The PREFACE.

who in their Printed Books and Accounts thereof, assume to themselves the Honour of both; Providence seeming to reserve the Glory of succeeding in so noble an Enterprize, to the Zeal and Industry of a Private Subject of England, which was Twice in vain attempted by Louis XIV. of France, the most ambitious and powerful Monarch of Europe.

BUT as the perfect Discovery of that great River, its Seven Mouths, and all the Coast of Carolana, on the Bay of Mexico, for at least 14 Degrees of Longitude, was then effected, and most of the Persons who were actually upon it, with their Journals, Drafts and Charts, return'd safe to England, the Proprietor presented a Memorial thereof to his then Majesty King William of Glorious Memory, wherewith He was so well pleas'd and satisfy'd, that in a General Council call'd for that Purpose, he order'd it to be read, and taken into Consideration, Himself, and above Twenty of the Council, who were then
present,

The PREFACE.

present, *unanimously agreeing,* that the Design *of* settling *the* said Province ought *to be* speedily *encourag'd and promoted.*

HIS *said* Majesty *being afterwards more fully convinc'd, that such an* Undertaking *would greatly tend to the* Benefit *of the* English Nation, *and the* Security *of its* Colonies *on the Continent of* North America, *often declar'd, that he would leap over* Twenty Stumbling-Blocks, *rather than not effect it ; and frequently assur'd the* present Proprietor, *that it should not only receive a* Publick Encouragement, *but that he would particularly contribute towards it,* by *sending at his own* Cost Six *or* Eight Hundred French Refugees *and* Vaudois, *to joyn with those* English *who could be procur'd to begin the* Settlement there.

BESIDES *divers* Noblemen, Gentlemen *and* Merchants, *proffer'd the same. Particularly the* Lord Lonsdale, *then* Lord Privy-Seal, *being highly sensible of the great* Advantages *would redound to the* English Nation *thereby,*

B 5   *offer'd*

The PREFACE.

offer'd to affift the Defign with Two
Thoufand Pounds in ready Mony, or a
Ship of Two Hundred Tuns, with
One hundred Perfons of whatfoever
Trades or Employments fhould be
thought moft convenient; and to provide
them with Provifions, neceffary Tools
and Inftruments, for the Space of One
Year; not making the leaft Capitulation
for himfelf or them, beyond the Grant
of a Competent Tract of Land for their
Habitation and neceffary Subfiftance:
But the fudden Death of that Lord,
and foon after of King William, put a
Period, at that Time, to this noble
Undertaking.

THE prefent Proprietor, not long after
the Death of that Monarch, did in the
fubfequent Reign propofe the reviving
and promoting the aforefaid Enterprize,
but the Wars enfuing, which prov'd ex-
ceffive chargeable, and employ'd the whole
Thoughts and Attention of the Mini-
ftry, hinder'd the encouraging thereof.
Whereupon he defifted from any further
Profecution of that Affair, till a fitter
Opportunity

The PREFACE.

Oportunity *should offer itself, though very sorry his* Country *had lost so favourable a* Conjuncture, *when what he had propos'd might have been accomplish'd with much less* Trouble *and* Expence, *than after a* Peace *should be concluded ;* for *he foresaw, and often warn'd the then* Ministry, *that whensoever that happen'd, the* French *would certainly endeavour to possess and settle that Country, for* Reasons *too many and tedious here to relate, as afterwards too manifestly appear'd.*

HOWSOEVER *as this* Colony *does most certainly of* Right *belong to the* Crown *of* Great-Britain, *if the first* Discovery, Grant, Possession, *and other most material* Circumstances, *may be allow'd to carry any* Weight *with them, it may be a satisfactory* Entertainment, *if not a real* Service, *to the* Publick, *to attempt a short* Description *of it in* Print, *and of the* Lands *to the* Northwards, *as far as, and among the* Five great Lakes, *the* Nations *of* Indians *inhabiting therein, and the* Lakes *themselves, as well as of the useful* Animals

The PREFACE.

nimals, Vegetables, Mettals, Mine-
rals, *and other the* Produce *thereof* ; *together with an* Account *of the great* River
Meſchacebe, *and the* Rivers *which increaſe it both from the* Eaſt *and the*
Weſt ; *as likewiſe a brief* Relation *of
the* Coaſt *of this* Province, *on the* Bay
of Mexico, *and the* Rivers, Harbors,
and Iſlands *belonging to it* ; *all which,
I flatter myſelf, are more particular and
exact than any* Thing *the* French *have
publiſh'd relating thereto. The ſame may
be ſaid of the annex'd* Map, *which no
doubt is the beſt of its* Kind *extant. By
both which the* Reader *will ſee, how
contiguous this* Province *lies to our already ſettled* Colonies, *which are entirely
ſurrounded by it, and the other* Lands
to the Northward, *by the* French *call'd*
Canada *or* New France, *tho' thoſe to
the* Southward *of the great* Lakes *they
moſt unjuſtly claim the* Property *of.*
For *they were, about the Beginning of
the Reign of King* James II. *made
over and ſurrender'd, by the* Irocois *and
their* Allies, *to the* Crown *of* England,

we

the Right *and* Poffeffion *whereof* we *have ever fince afferted and* endeavour'd *to fecure,* both *by* ourfelves *and the* abovefaid Indians *our* Confederates, *who on their* Parts, *on all* Occafions *of* Difference *with the* French *or their* Indians, *do for that and other* Confiderations, *demand the good* Offices *and* Protection *of the* Englifh, *who knowing it their* Intereft, *never fail, if the* Caufe *is juft, to afford it them:* As *they did in the* Year 1696. *When the* Count Frontenac Governour *of* Canada, *with feveral* Thoufand French *and* Indians, *attack'd the* Onondages, One *of the* Five Nations, *and* Ravag'd *their* Country; *but on the* Approach *of* Collonel Fletcher Governour *of* New-York, *with fome* Regular Forces, Militia *and* Indians, *he was forc'd to retire, not without a* confiderable Lofs *from thofe* Natives, *who conftantly attended him in his* Retreat, *often fell on his* Rear, *cut off many of his* People, *and all the* Straglers *they could meet with.*

THE

The PREFACE.

THE *Five Nations*, when *summon'd* on our two *laſt unfortunate Expeditions againſt* Canada, *readily join'd the* Engliſh *Troops under the Command of General* Nicholſon, *with about a Thouſand Men* ; *And the reſt of them were in Motion in different Parts* ; *ſome to diſcover and obſerve the Poſture of the Enemy in their own Country; Others to Scout about the* Rivers *and* Lakes. *And they have ſo great a Reliance on the* Friendſhip *and* Protection *of the* Engliſh, *whom they have ever found and acknowledg'd to be truly* Juſt, Honeſt *and* Punctual, *in their* Treaties *and* Dealings *with them, that during the late War, they not only permitted, but alſo invited them, to build a* Fort *in the very heart of their* Country *and on their* Main River, *the Gate of which adjoyns to and Opens into One of their* Capital Towns *or* Fortifications, *Inhabited by the* Mohacks, *the chief and moſt Warlike* Nation *among them. The* Engliſh *Garriſon being a* Detachment *from the* Independent Companies *of* New-York

The PREFACE.

York *and* Albany, *live with them in the* ſtricteſt Amity, *and dayly enter their* Caſtle *as the* Indians *do Our* Fort, *who conſtantly ſupply the'* Soldiers *with* Veniſon, Wild-Fowl, Fiſh, *and other* Neceſſaries *in their* Way.

FROM *theſe* Indians *of the* Five Nations, *the* Engliſh *of* New-York, *purchaſe the greateſt Part of their* Furr *and* Peltry-Trade, *and in* Exchange *ſupply them with* Duffels, Strowds, Blankets, Guns, Powder, Shot, *and other the* Manufactures *of* Great-Britain, *at a much eaſier Rate than the* French *ever could.*

THAT Nation *knowing and envying the great* Friendſhip *and* Commerce *the* Engliſh *of* New-York *cultivate and carry on with theſe* Indians, *and being ſenſible of the mighty* Uſe *and* Service *they are of, not only to that* Colony, *but to all our other* Colonies *to the* Northward, *have on, many* Occaſions *endeavour'd, by all the* Artifices *imaginable, to draw them over to their* Party *and* Intereſts, *which when they*

they fail'd in, *They have attempted*, *by*
Force *or* Fraud *to Extirpate or Subject
them :* But *that cunning and Warlike*
People, *by the Advice and Assistance
of the* English, *have ever prevented their*
Designs, *to whom they continue most
incens'd and irreconcileable* Enemies ;
tho' as long as the English *have* Peace
with them, *they are persuaded to continue the same.*

INDEED *during the Reign of* King
James II. *They had certainly been* Cut
off *and* exterminated *by the* French
(*the* English *being prohibited*, *to give
them the least Assistance*) *had not the
happy* Revolution *of* King William
intervened, *and the War with* France
soon succeeded.

NAY, *even Collonel* Dungan *a* Roman Catholick, *made Governour of*
New-York *by* King James, *was at
that Time so very sensible of the* Ruin
intended to the Five Nations *our* Allies,
and in Consequence to the English Plantations, *that he order'd the* Popish
Priests, *who were by* Leave *come into*
                                            his

his Government, *under* pretence of making Proselytes, *to depart from thence,* because he found their Design *was to betray* our Colonies *to the* French, *inſtead of making* Converts *of the* Inhabitants.

THE French, *as is related above, have many ways endeavour'd to ruin or diſtreſs the* Irocois; *but as they are well aſſur'd,* Nothing will affect them ſo much and nearly, *as to deprive them of their* Fiſhing and Hunting, *which is moſtly on the Borders of, and between the* Great Lakes, *and without which they muſt* Starve; *therefore they have attempted to build* Forts *on the ſeveral narrow* Paſſages *thereof, and the* Rivers *which empty themſelves thereinto, in order to intercept them, either in their going or returning from thoſe* Places; *but the* Indians *have as often prevented the finiſhing of them, or otherwiſe oblig'd them to demoliſh or deſert them.*

BUT *ſhould the* French *be permitted to eſtabliſh their projected* Communication, *between* Cape Breton *the* Gulf *and* River *of* St. Lawrence, *as far as the*

The PREFACE.

the Meſchacebe, *and ſo downwards to the* Bay *of* Mexico, *which will be a migh-ty* Addition *and* Increaſe *of* Territory, Strength *and* Power *to them, It is much to be fear'd, They'l carry their* Point *one Time or another, and thereby diſtreſs and Subject theſe our* Allies, *the Conſe-quence of which will not only be very* ſhocking, *but of the utmoſt* Concern *to the* Safety *of our* Northern Plantations*: For if we now, in ſo great Meaſure, ſtand in need of, and depend on them as our* Friends, *for the* Security *of our* Fron-tiers, *what muſt we expect, when that* Barrier *is remov'd, and they become our* Enemies; *and not only they, but all the* Reſt *of our Friendly* Indians *to the* South-ward, *which we may of* Courſe *depend on.*

WE *have lately experienc'd the* diſmal *and* Tragical Conſequences *attending a* Defection, *of only one or two* Paltry Nations *of* Indians, *bordering on* Caro-lina, *and though other* Pretences *have been urg'd as the* Cauſe *thereof, and were perhaps in ſome* Meaſure *true, yet the*

French,

The PREFACE.

French, *fince their late* Settlements *on*
the Meschacebe *and th*2 *Bay of* Mexico, *are violently fufpected to have* clan-
deftinely fomented and widen'd the Breach,
which occafion'd the butchering of fo ma-
ny hundreds *of the* Inhabitants *of that*
Colony, *with the* Burnings, Devafta-
tions, *and almoft* intire Defolation *there-*
of.

    IT *is well known that the* Frontiers
of our Colonies *are large,* naked, *and*
open, there being fcarce any Forts *or*
Garrifons *to defend them for near* Two
Thoufand Miles. *The* dwellings *of*
the Inhabitants *are fcattering and at a*
Diftance from one another; and its almoft im-
poffible according to the prefent Eftablifh-
ment *and* Scituation *of our* Affairs *there,*
from the great Number *of our* Colonies
independent on each other, their different
Sorts of Governments, Views, *and* In-
terefts, *to draw any confiderable Body*
of Forces *together on an* Emergency,
though the Safety *and* Prefervation, *not*
only of any particular Colony, *but of*
all the Englifh Plantations *on the Continent,*
were never fo nearly concern'd.   FOR

The PREFACE.

FOR, *several of these* Governments, *pretending to or enjoying some extraordinary* Privileges, *which the* Favour *of the* Crown *has formerly granted them, exclusive of others, if their* Assistance *is demanded or implor'd by any of their distress'd* Neighbours, *attack'd by* Enemies, *perhaps in the very* Heart *of their* Settlements, *they either by affected* Delays, *insisting on* Punctilios *and* Niceties, *starting unreasonable* Objections, *and making extravagant* Demands, *or other frivolous* Pretences, *purposely elude their just and reasonable* Expectations; *and by an inactive* Stupidity *or* Indolence, *seem insensible of their particular and most deplorable* Circumstances, *as well as regardless of the* General *or* Common Danger, *because they feel not the* immediate Effects *of it*; *Not considering their own* Security *is precarious, since what happens to one* Colony *to* Day, *may reach another to* Morrow: *A* Wise Man *will not stand with his* Arms *folded, when his* Neighbours House *is on* Fire.

THE

The PREFACE.

THE only Expedient *I can at pre-sent think of,* or *shall presume to mention (with the utmost* Deference *to His* MAJESTY *and His* Ministers) *to help and obviate these* Absurdities *and* Inconveniencies, *and apply a* Remedy *to them,* is, *That All the* Colonies *appertaining to the Crown of* GREAT BRITAIN *on the* Northern Continent *of* America, *be United under a* Legal, Regular, *and firm* Establishment; *Over which, it's propos'd, a* Lieutenant, *or* Supreme Governour, *may be constituted, and appointed to Preside on the* Spot, *to whom the* Governours *of each* Colony *shall be* Subordinate.

IT *is further humbly propos'd, That two* Deputies *shall be annually Elected by the* Council *and* Assembly *of each* Province, *who are to be in the Nature of a* Great Council, *or* General Convention *of the* Estates *of the* Colonies; *and by the* Order, Consent *or* Approbation *of the* Lieutenant *or* Governour General, *shall meet together, Consult and Advise for the Good of the*

c   *whole,*

The PREFACE.

whole, Settle *and* Appoint *particular*. Quota's *or* Proportions *of* Money, Men, Provisions, *&c. that each respe-ctive* Government *is to raise, for their mutual* Defence *and* Safety , *as well, as, if necessary, for* Offence *and* Invasion *of their* Enemies ; *in all which Cases the* Governour General *or* Lieutenant *is to have a* Negative ; *but not to Enact any Thing without their Concurrence, or that of the* Majority *of them.*

THE Quota *or* Proportion, *as above allotted and charg'd on each* Colony, *may, nevertheless, be levy'd and rais'd by its own* Assembly, *in such Manner, as They shall judge most Easy and Convenient, and the Circumstances of their Affairs will permit.*

OTHER Jurisdictions, Powers *and* Authorities, *respecting the Honour of His* MAJESTY, *the* Interest *of the* Plantations, *and the* Liberty *and* Property *of the* Proprietors , Traders , Planters *and* Inhabitants *in them, may be Vested in and Cognizable by the above-said*

The PREFACE.

said Governour General *or* Lieutenant, *and* Grand Convention *of the* Eſtates, *according to the* Laws *of* England , *but are not thought fit to be touch'd on or inſerted here* ; *This* Propoſal *being* General, *and withall humility ſubmitted to the Conſideration of our* Superiours, *who may* Improve, Model, *or* Reject *it, as they in their* Wiſdom *ſhall judge proper.*

A COALITION *or* Union *of this* Nature, *temper'd with and grounded on* Prudence, Moderation *and* Juſtice, *and a* generous Incouragement *given to the* Labour, Induſtry, *and* good Management *of all Sorts and* Conditions *of* Perſons *inhabiting, or, any ways, concern'd or intereſted in the ſeveral* Colonies *above mention'd,* will, *in all probability, lay a ſure and laſting* Foundation *of* Dominion, Strength, *and* Trade, *ſufficient not only to* Secure *and* Promote *the* Proſperity *of the* Plantations, *but to revive and greatly increaſe the late* Flouriſhing State *and* Condition *of* GREAT BRTITAIN, *and there-*

C 2 *by*

The PREFACE.

by render it, once more, the Envy *and* Admiration *of its* Neighbours.

LET *us consider the* Fall *of our* Ancestors, *and grow wise by their* Misfortunes. *If the Ancient* Britains *had been united amongst themselves, the* Romans, *in all probability, had never become their* Masters : *For as* Cæsar *observ'd of them,* Dum Singuli pugnabant, Universi vincebantur, *whilst they fought in seperate* Bodies, *the whole* Island *was subdued. So if the* English Colonies *in* America *were* Consolidated *as one* Body, *and joyn'd in one* Common Interest, *as they are under one* Gracious Sovereign, *and with* united Forces *were ready and willing to act in* Concert, *and assist each other, they would be better enabled to provide for and defend themselves, against any troublesome* Ambitious Neighbour, *or bold* Invader. *For* Union *and* Concord *increase and establish* Strength *and* Power, *whilst* Division *and* Discord *have the contrary* Effects.

BUT

The PREFACE.

BUT *to put a* Period *to this* Digreſſion; *It ſeems to me a very great* Indignity *offer'd to His* MAJESTY *and the* Nation, *that when there are* Five Hundred Thouſand *Britiſh* Subjects *(which are above five times more than the* French *have both in* Canada *and* Louiſiana *put together) inhabiting the ſeveral* Colonies *on the* Eaſt *ſide of the* Continent *of* North America, *along the* Sea Shoare, *from the* Gulf *of* St. Laurence *to that of* Florida, *all contiguous to each other, who, for almoſt a* Century, *have eſtabliſh'd a* Correſpondence, *contracted a* Friendſhip, *and carry'd on a flouriſhing* Trade *and* Commerce *with the ſeveral* Nations *of* Indians, *lying on their* Back, *to the* Weſtward *and* Northward, *for* Furs, Skins, &c. *a moſt rich and valuable* Traffick, *the* Colonies *themſelves abounding with* Metals *and* Minerals *of* Copper, Iron, Lead, &c. *producing* Hemp, Flax, Pitch, Tarr, Roſin, Turpintine, Maſts, Timber *and* Planks *of* Oak,

c 3   Fir,

The PREFACE.

Fir, *and all other sorts of* Naval Stores, *in great abundance, and the best of their Kind in the World; besides* Wheat, Beef, Pork, Tobacco, Rice, *and other necessary and profitable* Commodities; *with a Noble* Fishery *for* Whales, Codfish, &c. *along the* Coast *and in the* Bays *thereof, I say, it seems a great* Indignity *offer'd to His* MAJESTY *and the* British Nation, *that the* French *should seize on and Fortify this* Province *of* Carolana, *remote from* Canada *near a Thousand Miles, as well as the other* Lands *to the* Westward, *or on the Back of our* Settlements *(the greatest Part of which are comprehended in divers Patents granted long ago, by several of His* MAJESTY'S *Royal* Predecessors, Kings *and* Queens of England,) *Especially since the* English *have Planted and Improv'd them, from the* Sea Coast, *almost up to the* Sources *of the largest* Rivers, *by the* Consent *of the* Natives, *whose* Lands *they have actually purchas'd and paid for, and whose* Traffick *we are hereby intirely depriv'd of.*

MOREOVER

MOREOVER *if the* English *suffer themselves to be thus straitly coop'd up, without stretching their* Plantations *further back into the* Continent, *what will become of their* Off-spring *and* Descendants, *the Increase of their Own and the* Nations Stock, *who Claim and Demand an* Habitation *and* Inheritance *near their* Parents, Relations *and* Friends, *and have a* Right *to be provided for in the* Country *where they are Born, both by the Laws of* GOD *and* Man ; *and which the* Prudence *and* Policy *of the* State *does likewise require, as convenient and necessary, both for extending our* Territories, *strengthening our* Hands, *and enlarging our* Trade.

BESIDES, *as the* English *are not fond of extending their* Dominions *on the Continent of* Europe, *but confine themselves to their* Islands, *being content with their* Ancient Territories *and* Possessions, *except what is absolutly necessary to promote and secure their* Trade *and* Commerce, *the very* Vitals *of the* State, *I cannot apprehend with what* Reason *or* Justice

c 4

the

The PREFACE.

the French, *or any other* Nation, *should
encroach upon their* Claims, Colonys, *or*
Plantations *in* America.

THAT *They have done this is plain,
from the Accounts we continually receiv'd
from* France, *for many Years past, of the
several* Embarkations *for the* Meschacebe *or* Louisiana, *and the* Encouragement
given to their West-India Company, *for
the Planting and Raising* Materials *for*
Manufactures *therein.*

WE *have likewise been, with just
Reason, alarm'd here in* Great Britain,
by the many Letters, Memorials, Repre-
sentations *and* Remonstrances, *which
have, from Time to Time, been transmit-
ted, from divers of our* Colonies *upon the
Continent of* America, *setting forth the*
Danger *they are like to be expos'd to,
from the* Neighbourhood *of the* French,
if they obtain full Possession of this our
Province *of* Carolana, *and the Lands
to the* Northward *of it, as far as the
Five great* Lakes, *which comprehends
great Part of what they call* la Louisiane.

FOR

The PREFACE.

FOR *through these* Countries *many
great* Rivers *have their Course*, *proceeding
from the Back of our* Colonies *of* New
York, New Jersey, Pensilvania, Maryland, Virginia, North *and* South Carolina, (*their Springs being not far distant
from the Heads of the Chief* Rivers, *that
belong to and run through those* Colonies)
*most of them Navigable without Interruption
from their* Fountains, *till they fall into
the* Meschacebe. *And by means of their*
Settlements *on that and the other Inland*
Rivers *and* Lakes, *from the Bay of*
Mexico, *to the River and Bay of St.*
Laurence, *the* French *are drawing a
Line of* Communication, *and endeavouring to surround and streighten all our* Colonies, *from* Nova Scotia *to* South Carolina. *Thus are they working out their
own* Grandure *and Our* Destruction.

INDEED *the* French, *who all the World
acknowledge to be an Enterpizing, Great
and Politick* Nation, *are so sensible of the*
Advantages *of* Foreign Colonies, *both
in reference to* Empire *and* Trade, *that
they use all manner of* Artifices *to lull
their*

their Neighbours *a* ſleep, *with* Fine Speeches *and* plauſible Pretences, *whilſt they cunningly endeavour to compaſs their* Deſigns *by degrees, tho' at the hazard of encroaching on their* Friends *and* Allies, *and depriving them of their* Territories *and* Dominions *in Time of* Profound Peace, *and contrary to the moſt* Solemn Treaties.

FOR *beſides their ſeizing on, and ſetling the great* River Meſchacebe, *and ſome part of the* North Side *of the* Bay *of* Mexico, *and the claim they ſeem clandeſtinely to make to another of our inhabited* Southern Colonies *adjoyning thereunto, as I ſhall in the* Sequel *demonſtrate, they in ſome of their Writings boaſt, that their* Colony *of* Louiſiana, *hath no other Bounds to the* North *than the* Arctick Pole, *and that its Limits on the* Weſt *and* North Weſt *are not known much better, but extend to the* South Sea, Japan, *or where-ever they ſhall think fit to* Fix *them, if they can be perſwaded to fix any at all; intending thereby to deprive the* Britiſh Nation *of all that vaſt Tract*

of

The PREFACE.

of Land Situate between the Gulf of Mexico *and* HudſonsBay, *which includes this our Province of* Carolana, *the aforeſaid great* Lakes, *and the whole* Country *of our* Five Nations, *with the* Fur, Peltry, *and other* Trade *thereof. And what further Views and* Deſigns *they may entertain againſt the* Spaniſh *Provinces of* New Mexico *and* New Biſcay, *may be eaſily conjectur'd ſince the* World *has been certainly appriz'd of the* Project *fram'd by* Monſieur Dela Salle, *to* Viſit *and* Seize *on the Rich* Mines *of* St. Barbe, &c. *which if he thought no difficult* Task *to accompliſh, with about* Two Hundred French, *and the* Aſſiſtance *of the* Indians *adjoyning to, and in actual* War *with the* Spaniards, *how much more eaſily will they become* Maſters *of them, when with the* United Strength *of* Canada *and* Louiſiana, *both* French *and* Natives, *they ſhall think fit to attack them. And after ſuch an* Acquiſition *of the* Numerous Mines *of thoſe* Provinces, *with the* Immenſe Riches *thereof, what may not our* Colonies, *on the Continent of* America, *apprehend from them.* BE-

The PREFACE.

BESIDES Jamaica *lying, as it were, lockt up, between their Settlements in the* Island of Hispaniola, *and those on the* Bay of Mexico, *will soon be in Danger of falling into their Hands ; and whether the* Havana *itself, and the whole Island of* Cuba, *with the Key of* Old Mexico, La vera Cruz, *will long remain in the Possession of the* Spaniards, *is very much to be doubted. And supposing the best that can happen to us, it will be but* Ulisses's *Fate, to have the Favour of being destroy'd last :* A *very* Comfortable Consideration.

WE *are all sensible what Clamours were rais'd at the Concessions made to* France, *on the Conclusion of the late* Peace *at* Utrecht. *There's scarce a Man well vers'd in the Interest of* Trade *and* Plantations, *but blam'd the then* Ministry *for not insisting on the Surrender of* Canada, *as well as* Nova Scotia *and* Newfoundland, *for the Security of our* Northern Colonies *on the Continent of* America, *and the* Traffick *thereof :* Nor ought they to have allow'd them the Possession of Cape Breton, if they had well consider'd or under-*
stood

ſtood the Nature of the Fiſhery *in thoſe* Seas.

THE *Hiſtory of* former Ages, *and the Experience of theſe* latter Times *have inform'd us, that the* French *have ever been troubleſome* Neighbours, *whereſoever they were ſeated :* Hiſtorians *aſſerting, that the natural* Levity *and reſtleſsneſs of their* Temper, *their enterprizing* Genius, *and* Ambition *of extending their* Dominions, *and raiſing the* Glory *and* Grandeur *of their* Monarchs, *contribute in great Meaſure to make them ſo.*

WHEREFORE *it's to be hop'd, that the* Britiſh Nation, *will be ſo far from continuing idle or indifferent* Spectators *of the unreaſonable and unjuſt* Uſurpations *and* Encroachments *of the* French, *on the* Continent *of* America, *that they'll let 'em know, they have enough already of* Canada *and* Cape Breton, *and that it's expected they abandon their* New Acquiſitions *on the* Meſchacebe *and the* Bay *of* Mexico, *that* River *and* Country *belonging of* Right *to the Crown of* Great Britain. *And I believe it will ſcarce be deny'd, that at*

 pre-

present, whilst they are weak, and in the Infancy and Confusion of their Settlements in Louisiana, we have a much better Chance, and are in far happier Circumstances, to put in our Claim to, and dispute the Right and Possession of that and the other Land, above mention'd with them, than we shall be some Years hence, when they have augmented the Number of their Inhabitants, debauch'd the Natives to their Party, and further strengthen'd themselves, by securing, with Forts and Garrisons, the Passes of the Rivers, Lakes and Mountains, even tho' they should not have obtain'd any Advantage over the Spaniards, or inrich'd themselves with the Wealth of Mexico.

I must acknowledge, that in Case the British Nation, should be so far infatuated, as not to assert their Right to this so noble, and to them so useful and necessary a Colony, and endeavour to regain the Possession thereof, or secure, at least, so much of it, as lies on the Back of our Plantations, as far Westward as the Meschacebe, it will be much more eligible and

for

for their Interest, that the Spaniards *were Masters of it than the* French, *we not having so much Reason to apprehend the same danger, either to our* Colonies, Trade *or* Navigation, *from the First, as from the Last. Tho' I'm far from admitting the Cession of it to either of them, on any Terms whatsoever, without an absolute and apparent Necessity, which, I thank* GOD, *we are not yet reduc'd to, nor apprehensive of.*

AND *I am apt to think, that Prudence and Policy, will or ought to prompt us, to keep a Ballance of Power in* America, *as well as nearer Home; and that as we have, for above Thirty Years past, found it our Interest to check and put a stop to the growing* Power *of* France, *and set* Bounds *to their Dominions here in* Europe, *we shall not easily be induc'd to allow them to encroach on, and deprive us of our* Colonies *and* Plantations *in* America.

THE Spaniards *are said to be very uneasy at the so near Neighbourhood of the* French *on the* Meschacebe, *and are perhaps more jealous of the Consequences thereof than we are, tho' not more than we ought to be;*

and

and, it's prefum'd, that on a proper Appli-
cation and Incouragement, they'll joyn
with us to oppofe and difpoffefs them of
their Settlements there and on the Bay of
Mexico, leaft they render themfelves fole
Mafters of the Navigation thereof, and
with the Affiftance of the Indians, make
Irruptions into the very Heart of their
Colonies, attack their Towns, feize
their Mines, and Fortify and Maintain
themfelves therein.

AND perhaps I may not be in the wrong
to fuggeft, that the Spaniards will readily divide this Country with us, and
furrender all their Pretentions to whatfoever lies Eaftward of the Mefchacebe,
except St. Auguftin, on Condition the
French are oblig'd to remove thence
and retire elfewhere. And indeed
nothing feems more proper and rea-
fonable, than for that Great River to
be the fettl'd and acknowledg'd Boundary and Partition, between the Territories of Spain and Great-Britain, on the
Northern Continent of America, Nature
feeming to have form'd it almoft purpofe-
ly

The PREFACE.

ly for that End, as will be evident to those who shall give themselves the Trouble of viewing the annexed Map. And at the same Time They'll perceive how the French have worm'd themselves into a Settlement *between the* English *and* Spanish Plantations, *on Pretence of a Vacancy; and with an* Assurance *scarce to be parrallel'd, have set* Bounds *to the* Dominions *of both.*

PERHAPS *I may be suspected by some People of a* Design *to plead for a* War *with* France *under Pretence of asserting our* Right *to the abovemention'd* Colony *and* Lands *adjacent, at a Time, when, by Reason of the present unsettl'd* Posture *of our* Affairs *we are so unfit for it. But I protest a* Thought *of that* Nature *is so contrary to my* Intentions, *and so foreign to my* Inclinations, *that I heartily and sincerely wish, if consistent with our* Honour, Interest *and* Safety, *we may ever avoid one with that* Nation ; *But then it is reasonable to expect from them a due* Observance *and* Execution *of* Treaties, *particularly that of* Utrecht, *by which,*

d   1

The PREFACE.

I am inform'd, They are excluded from enjoying any Acquifitions, *They have made in* America *during the* Late War.

I WOULD *not willingly charge them directly with a* Violation *of that* Treaty, *fince their* Refentment *againft the* Spaniards *for a* Breach *of it, is fo frefh in our* Memories, *and the* War *commenc'd with them, on that* Account *fo lately terminated. Yet if its alledg'd, They have acted, with* Refpect *to* Treaties, *fincerely and without* Referve *on their* Part, *how comes it, that whilft we were* Glorioufly *and* Generoufly *risking our* Fleets *by* Sea *in* Europe, *at fuch a diftance from* Home, *at fo vaft an* Expence, *and even at the* Inftance *of* France *itfelf, only to preferve the* Sanction *of* Treaties, *and do* Juftice *to our* Allies, *They fhould clandeftinely apply their* Naval Force, *to feize on and deprive us of our* Trade *and* Territories *in* America, *and* Settle *and* Aggrandize *themfelves at our* Expence, *where they had no* Right,
and

The PREFACE.

*and even, as is suggested, contrary to
the most solemn* Engagements.

THIS *is certainly a* Treatment *most*
Unjust *and* Dishonourable *to the* British Nation, *which I should not have
mention'd, if the* Duty *I owe to my* Sovereign, *and the* Affection *I bear to my*
Country, *did not forbid me at such a*
Juncture, *and on so Important an* Occasion, *to be silent and unconcern'd.*

IF *we tamely submit to* Insults *and*
Injuries *of this* Nature, *without being
alarm'd, and taking the necessary* Steps
towards a speedy and effectual Redress
of them, shall we not seem Infatuated
and Wanting *to ourselves, be arraign'd
as* Felo de se, *and accounted, with good*
Reason, *the* Bubbles *of the* French?
Won't *a* Noble *and* Generous Struggle,
for the rescuing and preserving Our Honour, Our Dominions *and* Our Trade,
better become Us, *than a* Base *and* Cow-
ardly Submission *and* Surrender *of
them? Shall we neglect the* Means *our*
Safety *asks? Or shall we suspect that our*
Good *and* Potent Allies, *whose* Interest

and

and Welfare we have had ſo much at Heart, during the two Late Wars, for whom we have hazarded ſo much, and perform'd ſo many and ſo Great Things, ſuccour'd them in their Extremities, and ſav'd them from impending Ruin; and even by our Fleets and Armies, at a Vaſt Expence of Blood and Treaſure, aſſiſted them to Conquer and Poſſeſs whole Provinces and Kingdoms; And after all this and more, Can we imagine They'll abandon us to Inſults and Injuries, and quietly acquieſce in our Misfortunes and Diſtreſs, who have ſo Generouſly Aſſiſted them in, and Extricated them out of theirs? Nay, may we not rather ſuppoſe and expect, that in Honour and Gratitude, They'll exert themſelves, and fly to our Aſſiſtance, with all imaginable Chearfulneſs and Alacrity, if ſo be at the enſuing Treaty of Peace, which is ſaid to be near at hand, we are not afraid to Publiſh our Wrongs, and Demand our Rights?

ALL the Writings of the French give us to underſtand, how fond They have been

of

The PREFACE.

of this Colony *for Thirty Years paſt,*
and the great Advantages *They propoſed*
to themſelves thereby. And the better to
engage their late Great Monarch's Ambition *of being Renown'd in* Future Hiſtory, *in* Alluſion *to his* Name, *They*
ſtil'd *it* La Louiſiane, *and the* Meſchacebe, *the River of* St. Louis, *tho' at*
that Time, They had but one ſmall Stoc-
kadoed Fort, *above Two hundred Miles*
from the Northern, *and Seven or Eight*
Hundred Miles *from the* Southern
Bounds *of this* Province.

BY *what is before mention'd, and the*
ſeveral Writings, Charts, *and* Maps
of the French, *it is evident, to what a*
narrow Extent *of* Ground *They have*
confin'd *the* Engliſh Plantations. *And*
particularly in L'Iſles *Map, the beſt and*
moſt approv'd of any they have lately publiſh'd, *beſides many very* Remarkables
there is One, *which I cannot omit taking*
Notice of, *viz. That on the Part where*
They fix Carolina, *now and long ſince*
inhabited by the Engliſh, *They have* inſerted *this Memorable Paſſage,* Caroline

ainſi

The PREFACE.

ainſi nommez en l'honneur de Charles
IX, par les Francois qui la decouvri-
rent en prirent Poſſeſſion et s' eſtabli-
rent lan 15. Caroline *ſo nam'd in*
Honour of Charles *the* IXth, *by the*
French, *who diſcover'd, took Poſſeſſion*
of, and ſettl'd it in the Year 15.. *by*
which the Author *ſeems to intimate the*
Right *of his* Nation *to that* Province ;
who, if they are ſo Bold *already, in ſo*
Publick *a manner, to put in their* Claim,
to it, may, its to be fear'd, when they
think themſelves ſtrong enough, by Force
aſſert it.

But *howſoever theſe Things may hap-*
pen (*which I pray* God *may not in our*
Days) *the* Proprietor *of* Carolana *will*
have the Comfort *and* Satisfaction *of*
having diſcharg'd his Duty *to the* Publick, *in affording Matter for the following*
Sheets, *which I here offer to the* View
and Peruſal *of all true* Britains, *in hopes*
They may prove acceptable, and engage
their Attention *for the* Publick Good.

But *if the ſaid* Proprietor *after ſo*
great Trouble *and* Expence, *ſhould have*
the

the Mortification *to see all his* honeſt *and* well meant Endeavours *rejected, and the* Fruits *of his* Labour *and* Subſtance render'd Ineffectual, *and loſt both to his* Country, himſelf *and* Family, *and this* Noble Province *ſecur'd by the* French, *without a* Probability *of* Redemption, *he muſt ſit down with* Patience, *and bewail his own* Misfortunes, *and the* Infatuation *of his* Countrymen, *who, as they formerly refus'd the* Honour *of being the firſt* Diſcoverers *of* America, *when it was offer'd them by the great* Columbus, *in the Reign of King* Henry *the* VIIth. *do now ſlight and deſpiſe the* Poſſeſſion *of a* Country, *which is* One *of the* Fineſt *and* moſt Valuable *in that* Part *of the* World, *and in their* Power *to ſecure, at leaſt the greateſt* Part *of it.*

YET *notwithſtanding theſe his* unſucceſsful *and* diſcouraging Efforts, *it will appear and continue as a* Memorial *to* Futurity, *by the* Diſcoveries *and* Relations *here publiſh'd, and the* Petitions, Memorials, *and* Repreſentations *formerly by him preſented to King* WILLIAM

d 4 *and*

The PREFACE.

and succeding Ministries *relating thereunto* (*many of the* Things *he then foretold betng since come to pass*) *that he has* acted *the* Part *both of a* Friend *and* Prophet *of his* Country ; *and that had his Advice been taken*, *and* Measures *put in* Practice, *many of the* Inconveniencies (*to say no worse*) *that have already happen'd*, *and are like still to befall the* English Plantations *on the Continent of* Amercia *and the* Trade *thereof*, *as well as in* Consequence *of that of their* Mother *good* Old England, *from this* Establishment *of the* French *on the* Meschacebe *and the* Bay *of* Mexico, *would in all* Probability, *have been nipt in the Bud*, *and intirely prevented*.

WHAT *is yet to be done therein* (*and there is no doubt but something may be successfully attempted*) *must be left*, *with all due Submission*, *to the Wisdom of His* MAJESTY *and His* Councils, *who*, *it's presum'd*, *will not neglect so favourable a* Conjuncture, *as the ensuing* Congsres *or* Treaty *of* Peace, *to* assert *and maintain the* Right *of the* British Nation *to*

this

this Province *and the* Lands *adjacent,* *or at leaſt to whatſoever lies to the* Eaſt-ward *of the* Meſchacebe, *and on the* Back, *and contiguous to our already ſettled* Plantations, *whoſe* Welfare *and* Proſperity *depends intirely on our being* Maſters *thereof, or on our preventing the* French *from being ſo, which I am perſuaded is ſtill in our* Power, *and may be effected.*

THE Probability *of a* Communication *by* Water (*except about half a* Day's Land Carriage) *between the River* Meſchacebe *and the* South-Sea, *ſtretching from* America *to* Japan *and* China, *which is repreſented in the* Fifth Chapter *of the enſuing* Treatiſe, *with the great* Advantages *to be made thereof, deſerves to be well and duely conſider'd.*

I *have only given a ſhort and ſuccinct* Account *and* Diſcription *of ſome of the moſt uſeful* Animals, Vegetables, Mettals, Minerals, Precious Stones, *and other* Commodities, *which are* Naturally, *or may with* Induſtry *be produc'd in this our* Province, *with ſome particular* Remarks *thereon. As for thoſe which are merely rare,* *and*

The PREFACE.

land serve chiefly for Speculation and Amusement, I have not so much as touch'd upon them ; neither have I made any Observations upon the Manners, Customs or Religion of the Natives, as being foreign to my present Purpose.

PERHAPS I may be look'd upon as a Visionary, who represent such Advantages may accrue to a Country not yet by us fully Possess'd or Planted ; But it will not seem so Ridiculous or Incredulous to them, that consider the wonderful Progress the Spaniards made, who in a little above Thirty Years after their Discovery of the Empire of Mexico, Conquer'd that of Peru, and Part of Chili, from whence they bring such Immense Treasures unto Old Spain. Their Beginnings were Ten times more Contemptible and Improbable than what I suggest. However, tho' the Undertakings hereafter mention'd may be suspended, till these Parts are well Secur'd and Inhabited by the Subjects of Great Britain. I have discharg'd my Duty in representing to the Publick, what may be effected,

and

The PREFACE.

and how, when Opportunity shall present.

IF such Objections had prevail'd, we
had never got that Footing on the Continent of America as now we have. And
to say nothing of other Commodities,
how vast a Revenue doth Tobacco alone
bring unto the Crown, and how Staple
and Beneficial a Merchandize for Foreign Trade? Not to enlarge about the
Trade with our Islands, who by Sugar,
Cotton, Indico, and many other Commodities, besides their Traffick with the
Spaniards, bring a great Treasure to the
Nation. And the Circular Trade to
and from the Continent and Islands,
greatly increase our Shipping, Seamen,
and Wealth, perhaps as much as all the
Trade we have with the whole Commercial World besides. To which may be
added, that nothing is of greater Importance to Great Britain, than the Consumption of its Native Growths and
Manufactures, and what vast Quantities of them are sent to and expended in
our American Plantations, the Bills of
Entry

The PREFACE.

Entry, *and the* Custom-House Books *will inform us.*

BESIDES *the great quantities of* Masts, Pitch, Tarr, Rosin, Turpentine, Hemp, Flax, Timber, Plank, Deal Boards, *and other* Naval Stores, *which are brought home from thence, or, on due* Encouragement, *may be had and raised there, prove not only extremely Beneficial to* Great Britain *at present, but will be render'd much more so, on a* War *or* Misunderstanding *with any of the* Northern Potentates, *from whose* Territories *we usually Import them, and to whom we pay for the most Part,* ready Money *and* Bullion *for them, to the amount of several Hundred Thousand Pounds* per Annum, *which will be kept within the Kingdom, when once we are supply'd with those* Commodities *from our own* Colonies, *which with due* Encouragement *we soon may.*

FOR *Proof of which,* Experience *has taught us, that formerly on the passing the* Act *of* Parliament, *which encourages the making* Pitch *and* Tarr, *in our* Planta-

Plantations, *the* Defign *was foon put in* Practice, *and the End fully anfwer'd,* thofe Commodities *being in a few Years* rais'd *and* Imported *in fuch* Quantities, *as to fupply the* Demands *and* Necef-fities *of moft, if not all the* Shipping *of* Great Britain, *at much lefs than half the* Price, *they were fold for before.*

BY *about Fourteen Years* Refidence *on the* Continent *of* America, *and the* Obfervations *I have made of the* Pro-duce *and* Trade *of the feveral* Colonies *therein, the moft confiderable of which I have often vifited, I think I can eafily demonftrate, that there is not one* Com-modity *of any* Confequence, *which we have from* Rufia *or the* Baltick, *but may be found or rais'd there, and in as great* Quantities *and* Perfection. *So that if the* Nation *would intirely flight the* Trade *and* Navigation *of thofe* Countries, *and apply themfelves vigoroufly to the* Traffick *of our* Plantations, *they would foon find their* Account *in it, and gain by the* Change *Annually near, if not full,* Half a Million *of* Money; *befides refcuing*

rescuing ourselves from a sort of Dependance *on the* Northern Powers, *whose*
unreasonable Caprices *and* Impositions,
We have, to our *great* Discredit *and*
Detriment, *too long experienc'd.*

BUT *if the* French *should ever grow*
so Powerful *in* America, *as to be able*
to Intercept or Engross the Trade *with*
the Indians, *or Ruin or Subject our*
Plantations, *there's an End of this* Consumption *of our* Home Produce *and*
Manufactures, *of all our* Shipping
Trade *thither,* of the Customs *for*
Goods *Exported there or imported thence,*
the Increase *of our* Sailors, *and the*
Advantages *of raising our own* Naval
Stores ; *besides the Loss of so Large an*
Extent of Dominion, *and Five Hundred*
Thousand British Subjects *therein.* We
may likewise be assur'd that all our Islands
in the West-Indies, *will soon undergo the*
same Fate, *or be terribly distress'd, for*
want of their usual Supplies of Fish, Lumber *and other* Necessaries, *they con-*
stantly stand in need of, and receive from
our Plantations *on the* Continent ,
which

The PREFACE.

which neither Great Britain nor Ireland can affift them with, and which They purchafe with their Sugar, Rum and Maloffes ; the Vent of which will be in great meafure ftopt on the Lofs of our Colonies, whereby they'll be mightily difcourag'd and impoverifh'd, fo as to become an eafy Acquifition to any Ambitious and Powerful Invador.

Thus GREAT BRITAIN being depriv'd of its Subjects, Dominions and Trade in and to America, our Merchants will be ruin'd, our Cuftoms and Funds will Sink, our Manufactures will want Vent, our Lands will Fall in Value, and inftead of decreafing, our Debts will increafe, without the leaft Profpect of the Nation's emerging.

I have thought fit to fubjoin an Appendix at the End of the Book, containing a fhort Extract of the Grant from King Charles I. to Sir Robert Heath, of this our Province of Carolana, and the Veanis and Bahama Iflands. Together with an Additional Claufe, taken from the Reprefentation of the Right Honourable

The PREFACE.

rable *the* Lords Commiſſioners *for*
Trade *and* Plantations *to King* William,
ſignifying the Report *of the then Attorney
General,* Sir Thomas Trevro, *now the*
Right Honourable *the* Lord Trevor, *in
Favour of the Title of the Preſent* Propri-
etor *thereunto.*

I have likewiſe inſerted an Abſtract *of
the firſt and moſt material* Memorial *preſented by the ſaid* Proprietor *to* King
William, *being a* Demonſtration *of the
juſt* Pretenſions *of the King of* England
to the aboveſaid Province, *and of the preſent* Proprietary *under his* MAJESTY.

ALL *other* Proceedings *reſpecting the
ſaid* Province, *both in that* Prince's
Time, and ſince his Preſent MAJESTY's
Acceſſion to the Throne, *are purpoſely
omitted, leaſt I ſhould ſwell the* Bulk *of
this* Treatiſe *too much, and tranſgreſs
my own fix'd* Reſolution, *which was to
contract it into as narrow a* Compaſs *as
poſſibly I could.*

As to the Work *itſelf I have little to
ſay, farther,* Then *if the* Importance *of
the* Subject, *and* Deſign *of the* Author,

cannot

The PREFACE.

cannot affect the Attention, *and at-tract the* Esteem *of the* Reader, *I know nothing therein considerable enough to do it.*

I SHALL *only add, That the* Principal Motive *which engag'd me to compose both the* foregoing *and the* following Sheets, *was a* Desire *to inform the* Publick *of an* Affair *of the greatest* Consequence, *and which it concerns them so much to know; and to excite some* Worthy Patriots *to search into, and fully examine the* Present Circumstances *and* Condition *of our* Plantations, *least* Ruin *steals on them unawares, and they are undone before they are thought to be in* Danger. *Whether I may attain my* End *therein I know not; but of this, I am certain, That my* Endeavours *are truly* honest *and* sincere, *and design'd more for a* Publick Good, *than a* Private Emolument.

I HAD *almost forgot to inform the* Reader, *That my* Reason *for not describing that* Part *of the* Province *of*

e   CARO-

The PREFACE.

Carolana, *bordering on the* North *or* Atlantick Ocean, *which comprehends the greateſt Part of* Carolina, *was, becauſe it has been ſo often and ſo well perform'd already, in the ſeveral Prin-ted Accounts of that laſt mention'd* Colony, *to which I referr.*

THE

THE
CONTENTS.

CHAP.

The CONTENTS.

CHAP. IV.

CHAP. V.

CHAP. VI.

A

A
DESCRIPTION, &c.

CHAP. I.

A Description of the great and famous River Meschacebe or Missisippi, *the Rivers increasing it both from the East and West, the Countries adjacent, and the several Nations of* Indians *inhabiting therein.*

AROLANA and *Carolina* are two distinct tho' bordering Provinces, the East of *Carolana* joyning to the West of *Carolina.* The former was granted by Patent unto Sir *Robert Heath* in the Beginning of the Reign of King *Charles* I.

B   which

which said Sir *Robert* was the then Attorney-General, and by him convey'd unto the Earl of *Arundel*, from whom it came by mean Conveyances unto the present Proprietary.

This Province of *Carolana* is extended North and South from the River St. *Mattheo*, lying according to the Patent in 31 Degrees (tho' by later and more accurate Observations, it is found to lie exactly in 30 Degrees and 10 Minutes) unto the River *Paſſo Magno*, which is in 36 Degrees of Northern Latitude; and in Longitude from the Weſtern or *Atlantick* Ocean unto New *Mexico* now in Poſſeſſion of the *Spaniards*, which is in a direct Line above 1000 Miles, and were not inhabited by them, unto the *South-Sea*. It comprehends within its Bounds, the greateſt Part of the Province of *Carolina*, whoſe Proprietors derive their Claim and Pretenſions thereto, by Charters from King *Charles* II. about Thirty Years after the abovemention'd Grant to Sir *Robert Heath*.

The great River *Meſchacebe* runs through the midſt of this Country, having a Courſe almoſt directly North and South from its firſt Fountains, in about 50 Degrees of North - Latitude, to its diſimboguing into the Middle of the Gulph of *Mexico*. The Rivers that make this, which the *Spaniards* call'd *Rio-grand del Norte*, proceed about one half from the Weſt, the other from the Eaſt, ſo that the whole Country may be almoſt

almoſt entirely viſited by Navigable Rivers without any Falls or Cataracts, which are uſual in moſt of the Northern Rivers of *America*, and in all Rivers of Long-Courſe, even in *Carolina*, (tho' to this Country contiguous) and thence Northward to the great River of St. *Laurence* or *Cannada*, and other Rivers Northward innumerable. The excellent and convenient Situation of this Country for Inland Trade and Navigation, and for Trade with the *Spaniards* in *New Mexico*, the whole Gulph of *Mexico*, and the *South-Sea* (which I ſhall hereafter demonſtrate) will be greatly for the Advantage, and not in the leaſt to the Prejudice of our Home Plantation Trade , as will appear more evident by the Deſcription of this great River *Meſchacebe*, and thoſe Rivers that enter into it, together with the vaſt Navigable Lakes of freſh Water adjoyning thereunto.

We will for good Reaſons begin our Deſcription of it from its Entrance into the Sea , aſcending up unto its Source ; and from very good Journals both by Sea and Land, give an Account of the Chief Rivers that run into it from the Eaſt and Weſt, as we find them in our Aſcent, together with their Courſe, Length and Bigneſs, the Nature of the Countries, and the Names of the Nations through which they paſs.

B 2   The

The River *Meschacebe* is so call'd by the
Inhabitants of the North; *Cebe*, being the
Name for a River, even as far as *Hudson's*
Bay; and *Mescha*, great, which is the great
River; And by the *French*, who learn'd it
from them, corruptly, *Missisippi*; which
Name of *Meschacebe* it doth retain among
the Savages, during half its Course: Afterwards some call it *Chucagua*, others *Saffa-
goula*, and *Malabanchia*, as it fares with the
Danubius, which 400 Miles before it enters
the *Euxine* Sea, is stil'd the *Ister*; and the
like happens to all the Rivers of Long
Course in *America*, as *Oronogue*, the River
of the *Amazons*, and *Rio de la Plata*. This
River enters the Gulph of *Mexico* 140 Leagues from the North West Part of the *Peninsula* of *Florida*, keeping along the Coast
in 30 Degrees North Latitude, and 120
Leagues from the most westerly Part of the
said Gulph in about 29 Degrees the same
Latitude; and thence the Coast extends S.
and by W. to the River *Panuco*, which is
under the *Tropick of Cancer* in 23½ Degrees,
the utmost Part inhabited by the *Spaniards*
towards the N. and N. E. on the Gulph of
Mexico.

The Province of *Carolina*, from the Conjunction with the *Peninsula* of *Florida*, for
250 Leagues is situated about the 30th Degree of North Latitude, and seldom varies
10 Leagues N. or S. from the same; excepting the Entrance of the River *Meschacebe*,

cebe, which I am now about to defcribe from the Mouth unto its firft Fountains.

The River *Mafchacebe* empties itfelf into the Gulph of *Mexico* by feven Channels like the River *Nile*, of which *Herodotus* the Father of Hiftory, and who liv'd long in *Egypt*, affirms in his Time, three were always Navigable, and the others only fo during the Inundations of the faid River, which were made by Art and Labour, tho' our Modern Navigators allow only two; but our River hath Seven Navigable at all Times; the Three great Ones by Ships, the Four fmaller, Two on each fide (as appears by the Chart) by Boats and Sloops, efpecially during the Time of the Waters rifing or the Frefhes, as they call them, which are always conftant, and return in the Spring, and fometimes happen in the Summer upon the great Rains, which is not frequent.

The Three great Branches always Navigable by Shipping, are fituated about 6 Miles diftant from each other, and unite all at one Place with the main River, about 12 Miles from their Mouths.

There is not above 14 Foot on the Barr at Low-Water in Neep-Tides, excepting when the Frefhes come down in the Spring or upon great Rains, but when you are over the Barr, which is not in many Places above a Ship's length Broad, you enter immediately

B 3

mediately into deep Water , the least 5
Fathom, which increases to 10 Fathom before you come to the main River : After
that it deepens gradually, to above 30, and
you have no where less than 20 Fathom
for a 100 Miles, and little less for 100
Leagues, and afterwards from 10 to 17 for
100 Leagues more : Then from 6 to 10,
200 Leagues further ; thence to the great
Cataract or Fall which is 1600 Miles from
its Entrance into the Sea, from 3 Fathom
to 6 : Its Breadth is generally during its
great Depth scarce a Mile, but as it lessens
in Depth, it encreases in Breadth, and is in
most Places of its Course Two Miles broad,
and where it makes Islands (as it does very
frequently) from the Middle of its Course
2 or 3 Leagues. The Banks in most
Places are no more than 5, or 6 Feet a-
bove the River, and Ships may almost in
all Places lie by the side of the Shore, there
being generally from 3 to 6 Fathom, and
deepens gradually , as you approach the
Middle of the River , which hath mostly
a pretty strong Current, but there are divers Promontories, under which you may
Anchor, where is good Shelter from Winds,
and curious Eddy-Tides.

When you are ascended the River 4 or
5 Leagues, it is border'd on each side with
high Trees of divers Sorts, from half a
Mile to 2 Miles deep into the Country,
very little under Woods, no Trouble in tra-
velling

velling, befides what procceds from the
Vines ramping upon the Ground. Divers
others furround and mount up the Trees,
almoft unto their Tops, which are feldom
lefs than 100 Feet from their Roots, and
often 30, or 40 Feet more. When you
come out of the agreeable Shade, you fee
a moft beautiful level Country, only about
6 or 8 Miles diftance, there are Collins or
gentle Afcents, for the moft Part round or
oval, crown'd with ftately Trees, which
looks more like a Work of laborious con-
fummate Art than of mere Nature ; and
this on both fides the River, fo far as the
acuteft Sight can reach ; in which Meadows
the wild Bulls and Kine, befides other Beafts,
graze, and in the Heat of the Day retire
into thefe Woods for Shelter, where they
chew the Cudd.

There is no confiderable River empties
itfelf into the *Mefchacebe* from the Mouths,
until you come about 12 Miles above the
Bayogola and *Mougolaches*, two Nations who
dwell together on the Weft-fide thereof,
200 Miles from the Sea ; then on the Eaft
fide, there falls out of the *Mefchacebe* a
Branch, which after a Courfe of 160 Miles,
empties itfelf into the N. E. End of the
great Bay of *Spirito Santo* ; it is not above
40 or 50 Yards broad, and 2 or 3 Fathom
deep at its beginning ; but foon enlarges
in Breadth and Depth by the Acceffion
of divers Rivers and Rivulets, and is a

moft

moſt lovely River, making pleaſant Lakes, and paſſing, during its whole Courſe, thro' a Country exactly like that we have formerly deſcrib'd : It is Navigable by the greateſt Boats, Sloops, and ſmall Ships of *Engliſh* Building ; and by large Ones , if built after the *Dutch* manner with flat Bottoms.

On the North-ſide of one of the abovemention'd Lakes, call'd by the *French* Lake *Pontchartrain*, they have erected a ſmall Fort, and Storehouſes, whither after unloading their large Veſſels at Iſle *aux Vaiſſeaux*, or Ships Iſland, they bring the Goods in Sloops or Shallops, and from thence diſperſe them by their Traders amongſt their own Settlements and the ſeveral Nations of *Indians*, inhabiting on and about the *Meſchacebe*, and the Rivers which enter it, both from the Eaſt and Weſt.

About 50 Miles above the Place where this River is diſmiſs'd from the *Meſchacebe*, on the other ſide, *viz.* the Weſt, enters the River of the *Houmas* ſo nam'd from a conſiderable Nation, who inhabit upon it in the Country, 6 or 8 Miles from its Mouth. This is a mighty River deep and broad, and comes from the Mountains of *New Mexico*; its Courſe is moſtly N. W. and is Navigable by large Veſſels above 300 Miles, and thence by large Boats and Sloops almoſt unto its Fountains. By this River you may have Communication with above 40 Nations,

ons, who live upon it, or its Branches; and also with the *Spaniards* of *New Mexico,* from whom its furtheft Heads are not above an eafy Day's Journey. Upon this River and moft of its Branches, are great Herds of wild Kine, which bear a fine Wooll, and Abundance of Horfe, both wild and tame of the *Spanifh* Breed, on which the *Indians* Ride, with almoft as much Skill as the *Europeans,* tho' the Bridles, Sadles, and Stirrups are fomewhat different from ours, yet not the lefs commodious.

Twelve Leagues Higher upon the River *Mefchacebe,* is the River of the *Naches,* which, 10 or 12 Leagues above its Mouth, divides itfelf into two Branches, and forms an Ifland about 30 Miles in Circumference, very pleafant and fertile. The South Branch is Inhabited by the *Corroas,* the North by the *Naches,* both confiderable Nations, a-bounding in all Neceffaries for Humane Life. Some Leagues above the Divifion is a pretty large Lake, where there is a great Fifhery for Pearl, large and good, taken out of a Shell-Fifh of a middle Nature between an Oyfter and a Mufcle.

About 12 or 14 Leagues higher on the fame, that is the Weft fide, the *Mefchacebe,* makes a little Gulph about 20 Miles long and 3 or 4 broad, upon which Inhabit in many Towns the Populous and Civilized Nation of the *Tahenfa,* who alfo abound in Pearls, and enjoy an Excellent Country ;

try; Are very hofpitable to Strangers, and tho' as moft *Indian* Nations, at War with there Neighbours, yet together with the three laft mentioned, and thofe to be here-after named, joyfully receive and kindly entertain all with whom they have not actual Hoftilities.

Fourteen or Fifteen Leagues higher on the Eaft fide of *Mefchacebe*, is the Nation and River of *Yafoue* which comes two or 300 Miles out of the Country, on which dwell the Nations in order mention'd after the *Yaffouees*, the *Tounicas*, *Kourouas*, *Tihiou*, *Samboukia* and *Epitoupa*.

Ten or 12 Leagues higher on the Weft Side, is the River *Natchitock*; which has a Courfe of many Hundred Miles: And after; it is Afcended about one hundred, there are many Springs, Pitts, and Lakes, which afford moft Excellent common Salt in great Plenty, wherewith they Trade with Neighbouring Nations for other Commodities they want, and may be of great Service to the *European* Inhabitants of this Country, to preferve Flefh, and Fifh for their own Ufe, and Exportation to Natives, *Spaniards*, and our Iflands, to the great Profit of them, who have not Stock to engage in greater and more beneficial Undertakings. Upon this River inhabit not only the *Nachitocks*, *Naguateeres*, *Natfchocks*, but higher feveral other Nations.

Sixteen

Sixteen Leagues further upon the Weſt ſide, enter the *Meſchacebe* two Rivers, which unite about 10 Leagues above, and make an Iſland call'd by the Name of the *Torimans*, by whom it is inhabited.

The Southerly of theſe two Rivers, is that of the *Ouſoutiwy* upon which dwell firſt the *Akanſas*, a great Nation, higher upon the ſame River the *Kanſa*, *Mintou*, *Erabacha* and others.

The River to the North is nam'd *Niska*, upon which live Part of the Nation of the *Ozages*; their great Body Inhabiting a large River which bears their Name, and Empties itſelf into the Yellow River, as will be hereafter mention'd: And upon this River near the Mouth is the Nation *Tonginga*, who with the *Torimans* are Part of the *Akanſaes*.

Ten Leagues higher is a Small River named *Cappa*, and upon it a People of the ſame Name, and another called *Oueſperies*, who fled, to avoid the Perſecution of the *Irocois*, from a River which ſtill bears their Name to be mention'd hereafter.

Ten Miles higher, on the ſame ſide of the *Meſchacebe*, is a little River nam'd *Matchicebe* upon which dwell the Nations *Matchagamia* and *Epiminguia*; over againſt whom is the great Nation of the *Chicazas*, whoſe Country extends above forty Leagues to the River of the *Cheraguees*, which we ſhall
describe

deſcribe when we come to Diſcourſe of the
great River *Hohio*.

Ten Leagues higher on the Eaſt ſide is
the River and Nation of *Chongue*, with ſome
others to the Eaſt of them.

Fifteen Leagues higher, on the Weſt ſide,
is the River and Nation of *Sypouria*.

Thirty Leagues higher on the Eaſt ſide,
is the opening of a River that proceeds
out of a Lake 20 Miles long, which is a-
bout 10 Miles from the *Meſchacebe*. Into
this Lake empty themſelves four large Rivers : The moſt Northerly, which comes from
the North Eaſt, is called *Ouabachicou* or
Ouabache upon which dwelt the Nations *Cha-
chakingua*, *Pepepicokia*, *Hohio*, *Pianguichia*. The
next South of this, is the vaſt River *Hohio*,
which comes from the back of *New-York*,
Maryland, and *Virginia*, and is Navigable
600 Miles. *Hohio* in the *Indian* Language
ſignifies the fair River ; And certainly it
runs from its Heads through the moſt Beautiful fertile Countries in the Univerſe, and
is form'd by the Confluence of 10 or 12
Rivers, and innumerable Rivulets. A Town
ſettled upon this Lake , or the Entrance
of the River *Hohio* thereinto, would have
Communication with a moſt lovely Fruit-
full Country 600 Miles Square. Formerly
divers Nations dwelt on this River as the
Chawanoes, a mighty and very populous People, who had above 50 Towns, and many other Nations who were totally deſtroy-
ed,

ed, or driven out of their Country by the *Irocois*; this River being their ufual Road when they make War upon the Nations who lie to the South or to the Weft.

South of the *Hohio* is another River which about 30 Leagues above the Lake is divided into two Branches; the Northerly is call'd *Ouefpere*, the Southerly the Black River, there are very few People upon either, they having been deftroy'd or driven away by the aforemention'd *Irocois*. The Heads of this River proceed from the Weft fide of the vaft Ridge of Mountains, which run on the Back of *Carolina*, *Virginia*, and *Maryland*; on whofe oppofite or Eaft fide, are the Sources of the great River *Potomack*, which by a Mouth of fome Leagues broad, difgorges itfelf into the middle of the Bay of *Chefepeack*, and feparates the two laft mention'd Provinces from each other. The Mountains afford a fhort Paffage or Communication between thofe two Rivers, which the *Indians* are well acquainted with, and by which in Conjunction with the *French* of the *Mefchacebe*, they may in Time infult and harrafs thofe Colonies.

The moft Southerly of the abovefaid four Rivers, which enter into the Lake, is a River fome call *Kafqui*, fo nam'd from a Nation Inhabiting a little above its Mouth; others call it the *Cufates* or the River of the *Cheraquees*, a mighty Nation, among whom it hath its chief Fountains; it comes from the
South

South Eaſt, and its Heads are among the Mountains, which ſeparate this Country from *Carolina*, and is the great Road of the Traders, from thence to the *Meſchacebe*, and intermediate Places. Above 200 Miles up this River to the South Eaſt, is the great and powerful Nation of the *Chicazas*, good Friends to the *Engliſh*, whoſe Dominion extends thence to the *Meſchacebe* : Before you come at them, is a ſmall Fall or Cataract, the only one I have yet heard of, in any of the Rivers that enter the *Meſchacebe*, either from the Eaſt or from the Weſt. Thirty or Forty Leagues above the *Chicazas*, this River forms four delicate Iſlands which have each a Nation Inhabiting them, *viz. Tahogale*, *Kakigue*, *Cochali*, and *Tali*. Sixty Leagues above the Iſland and Nation of the *Tali*, inhabits the aforemention'd Nation of the *Cheraquees*, who have at leaſt 60 Towns, ſome of which are not above 60 Miles from *Carolina*. They have great Friendſhip with the *Engliſh* of that Province, who from thence carry on a free Trade with, and are always very kindly entertain'd by them.

Fifteen Leagues above the *Hohio*, or the River coming out of the Lake aforemention'd, to the Weſt, is the River *Honabanou*, upon which dwells a Nation of the ſame Name, and another call'd *Amicoa* : And 10 Leagues above that, is the great Iſland of the *Tamaroas*, and over againſt it on the Eaſt ſide a Nation which goes by its Name, and another

other by that of *Cahokia* who dwell on the Banks of the River *Chepuſſo*..

Fifteen Leagues above which to the Weſt is the Great Yellow River, ſo nam'd becauſe it is Yellowiſh and ſo muddy, That tho' the *Meſchacebe* is very clear where they meet, and ſo many great Rivers of Chriſtaline water below, mix with the *Meſchacebe*, yet it diſcolours them all even unto the Sea. When you are up this River 60 or 70 Miles, you meet with two Branches. The leſſer, tho' large, proceeds from the South, and moſt of the Rivers that compoſe it falls from the Mountains, which ſeparate this Country from New *Mexico* ; notwithſtanding which, there is a very eaſie Communication between them. This is called the River of the *Orages*, from a Numerous People, who have 16 or 18 Towns ſeated thereupon, eſpecially near its mixing with the Yellow River. The other which is the main Branch, comes from the North Weſt, moſt of whoſe Branches deſcend likewiſe from the Mountains of *New Mexico*, and Divers other large Provinces which are to the North of *New-Mexico*, wholly poſſeſſed by *Indians*, who are ſaid to be very Numerous, and well polic'd : They are all at War with the *Spaniards*, from whom they have defended their Countries above 150 Years, and have rather recovered than loſt Ground. They are likewiſe at War, as generally the *Indians* are, amongſt themſelves.

felves. The moſt Northerly Branches of this River, are interwoven with other Branches, which have a contrary Courſe, proceeding to the Weſt, and empty themſelves into a vaſt Lake, whoſe Waters by means of another great River, diſembogues into the South-Sea. The *Indians* affirm, they ſee great Ships ſailing in that Lake, Twenty times bigger then their Canows. The Yellow is called the River of the *Maſſorites*, from a great Nation inhabiting in many Towns near its juncture with the River of the *Ozages* : There are many other Nations upon the ſame, little inferior to them in Extent of Territories or number of Towns, as the *Panimaha's, Pancaſſa's Pana's, Paneloga's, Matotantes*, few of them having leſs than 20 Towns, ſcarce any of which count leſs then 200 Cabans.

Forty Miles above the Yellow River, on the Eaſt ſide is the River *Checagou* or the River of the *Alinouecks*, corruptly by the *French* call'd *Illinois*, which Nation liv'd upon and about this River, having above 60 Towns, and formerly conſiſted of 20000 fighting Men, but are now almoſt totally deſtroy'd by the *Irocois*, or driven beyond the *Meſchacebe* Weſtward. This is a large Pleaſant River ; And about 250 Miles above its Entrance into the *Meſchacebe*, it is divided into two Branches; the leſſer comes from North and by Eaſt, and its Head is within 4 or 5 Miles of the great Lake of the *Alinouecks*

nouecks on its Weſt-ſide ; the other comes almoſt directly from the Eaſt, and proceeds
from a Moraſſe within 2 Miles of the River *Miamiha*, which empties itſelf into the
ſame Lake. On the South-Eaſt-ſide, there
is an eaſy Communication between theſe
two Rivers, by a Land-Carriage of 2 Leagues,
about 50 Miles to the South-Eaſt of the
foremention'd Lake. The Courſe of this
River from its Head exceeds 400 Miles,
Navigable above half way by Ships, and
moſt of the reſt by Sloops, and large Boats
or Barges. Many ſmall Rivers run into it,
and it forms 2 or 3 Lakes ; but one mightily extoll'd, call'd *Pimiteoüi*, which is 20
Miles long, and 3 Miles broad ; it affords
great Quantities of good Fiſh, and the
Country round about it, abounds with Game,
both Fowls and Beaſts. Beſides the *Illicoueck*,
are the Nations *Prouaria*, the great Nation
Caſcaſquia and *Caracontauon* ; and on the
Northern Branch inhabit Part of the Nation
of the *Maſcontens*.

On the South Eaſt Bank of this River,
Monſieur *de la Sale* erected a Fort in the
Year 1680, which he nam'd *Creve-caure*,
from the Grief which ſeiz'd him, on the
Loſs of one of his chief trading Barks rich-
ly laden, and the Mutiny, and villanous Intrigues of ſome of his Company, who firſt attempted to poyſon, and afterwards deſert him.
This Fort ſtands about half Way between

C   **thereof**

the Bay of *Mexico* and *Canada*, and was formerly the ufual Rout of the *French* in going to or returning from either of thofe Places: But fince they have difcover'd a nearer and eafier Paffage by the *Ouabache* and *Ohio*, the Sources of both which Rivers, are at a fmall Diftance from the Lake *Erie*, or fome Rivers which enter into it.

Forty Leagues higher on the Weft-fide is a fair River, which our People were at the Mouth of, but could not learn its Name. I fuppofe its the fame the *French* call *Moingona*. Some make it to proceed from the *Mitchayowa* or long River, as may be difcern'd in the annex'd Map; but as all our Journals are filent in that Matter, fo fhall I, till fome more perfect Difcoveries thereof afford us further Light and Certainty therein.

When you are afcended about 40 Leagues more; then on the Eaft-fide, falls into the *Mefchacebe*, the River *Mifconfiag*. This is much of the fame Nature with that of the *Alinouecks*, whether you confider its Breadth, Depth and Courfe; as alfo the Pleafantnefs, and Fertility of the Country, adjacent unto all its Branches. After you have row'd or fail'd up it 60 Miles, joyns with it, the River of the *Kikapouz*, which is alfo Navigable, and comes a great Way from the North-Eaft. Eighty Miles further, almoft directly Eaft, there is a ready Communication,

cation, by a Carriage of 2 Leagues, with the River of *Miscouaqui*, which hath a quite contrary Course, running to the North-East, and empties itself, after a Passage of 150 Miles from the Land Carriage, into the great Bay of the *Pouteouotamis*, or the *Puans*, which joyns, on the North-West, with the great Lake of the *Alinouecks*. This River and Bay I shall have Occasion to mention, when I come to describe the vast Lakes, or Seas of Fresh-Water, which are to the East of the *Meschacibe*.

Forty Leagues higher, on the same Side, is the fair large River *Mitchaoywa*, which is the same the *Barron le Hontan*, calls the long River, and gives a very particular Description thereof, having navigated it almost to its Heads. It has a Course of above 500 Miles, and the Southern Rivers, of which it is compos'd, are near the Northern Heads of the River of the *Messourites*, both taking their Original from the Mountains, which divide this Country, from that which leads to the *South Sea*. Several Rivers proceed from the other side of the Mountains, which are easily pass'd in less than one Day, and fall into the same Lake abovemention'd, which discharges itself by a great River into the aforesaid Sea. As you ascend this River from the *Meschacibe*, you meet with the Nations *Eokoro's*, *Essanape*, *Gnasitaries*, who have each many Towns, and very populous. And the said *Baron* acquaints us, from very good Information,

mation, That beyond these Hills, are Two
or Three Mighty Nations, under Potent
Kings, abundantly more civiliz'd, numerous,
and warlike, than their Neighbours, differing greatly in Customs, Buildings, and Government, from all the other Natives of this
Northern Continent : That they are cloathed, and build Houses, and Ships, like *Europeans*, having many of great Bigness, in
length 120 or 130 Foot, and carry from 2,
to 300 Men, which navigate the great Lake,
and it is thought the adjacent Parts of the
Ocean. And *Herrera*, *Gomara*, and some
other *Spanish* Historiographers assert, that the
Spaniards saw, upon that Coast, such Ships,
which they apprehended, came from *Japan*
or *China*.

A little higher up is the River *Chabadeba*,
above which the *Meschacebe* makes a fine
Lake, 20 Miles long, and 8 or 10 broad.

Nine or 10 Miles above that Lake, on
the East-side, is a large fair River call'd
the River of *Tortoises*, after you have entered a little Way, which leads far into the
Country to the North-East, and is navigable by the greatest Boats 40 Miles. About
the same Distance further up, the *Meschacebe*
is precipitated from the Rocks about 50
Foot, but is so far Navigable by considerable Ships, as also beyond, excepting another
Fall 80 or 90 Miles higher, by large Vessels
unto its Sources, which are in the Country of the *Sieux*, not at a very great Distance

ftance from *Hudfon*'s Bay. There are many
other fmaller Rivers which fall into the *Mefchacebe*, on both Sides of it, but being of
little Note, and the Defcription of them of
fmall Confequence, I have pafs'd them over
in Silence.

CHAP. II.

*A Defcription of the Coun-
tries, People, Rivers, Bays,
Harbours and Iflands, to the
Eaft of the* Mefchacebe,
*which do not communicate
with it.*

I NOW proceed to defcribe that Part
of this Province, which is to the Eaft
of the *Mefchacebe*; the Rivers, which
pafs through it, having no Communica-
tion therewith. From the *Peninfula* of
Florida, where this Country begins, to the
South-Eaft, there are only two large Rivers:
The Firft that of *Palache*, the true *Indian*
Name, by the *Spaniards* call'd the River of
Spirito

Spirito Santo or of *Apalache*, adding an *A*, after the *Arabian* manner, from which a great Part of their Language is deriv'd ; as in the Provinces of *Nilco*, *Minoia*, they pronounce *Anilco*, and *Aminoia*, and so in divers others. This River enters the Gulph of *Mexico* about 100 Miles from the Cod of the Bay of *Palache*, at the North-West End of the *Peninsula* of *Florida*, in 30 Degrees of North Latitude, and some few Minutes. It is somewhat hard to find, by Reason of the Isles and *Lagunes* before it ; and though a stately River, and comes far out of the Country, hath not above 2 Fathoms and a half, or 3 Fathoms Water at most on the Barr, as the People sent on Discovery found ; but that being pass'd its very deep and large ; and the Tide flows higher than into any other River upon all the Coast, some affirm 50 Miles, which is no wonder, the Country being a perfect Level, and the River having a double Current ; one from the South, all along the *Peninsula*, from 25 Degrees to 30 : The other from the West. Near it, on both Sides towards the Sea-Coast, dwell divers Nations, *Palachees*, *Chattoes*, *Sulluggoes*, *Tommakees*, &c ; who are generally call'd by one Name of *Apalatchy Indians*. This River proceeds chiefly from Rivers, which have their Origin on the South or South-West side of the great Ridge of Hills, that divides this Country from *Carolina*, and is suppos'd to have a Course of about 400 Miles.

Miles. Upon or near the Middle of it live the great Nations of the *Cufshetaes*, *Tallibou-fies* and *Adgebaches*.

To the West of this, is the famous *Coza*, or as ours call it the *Couffa* River, and the *French Mobile*, the biggest, next unto *Mefchacebe*, and *Hohio*, of any in this, or the Neighbouring Provinces. Its first Heads are likewise from the aforesaid *Palacheau* Mountains. The most Northerly being at *Gnaxula* Town and Province, near the Foot of the Mountain. Many Rivulets uniting, after a Course of 80 Miles, form a River bigger than the *Thames* at *Kingston*, making several delicious Isles, some 3, or 4 Miles long, and Half a Mile broad; the Country is wonderful pleasant and fertil. The first considerable Town or Province is *Chiaha*, famous for its Pearl-Fishing, there being thereabouts, in the River and little Lakes it makes, a Sort of Shell-Fish, the Ancients nam'd *Pinna*, between a Muscle and Oyster; concerning which I have discours'd in the Account of the Produces or Commodities of this Country. From thence the River grows larger and deeper, by Accession of others from the Mountains, and from the West, until it enters the Province of *Coza*, or *Couffa*, which is reckon'd one of the most pleasant and fruitful Parts of this Country, and very populous. Through this *Ferdinando Soto* pass'd, and resided therein a considerable Time; and all the *Spanish*

C 4   Wri-

Writers of this famous Expedition, extoll them above any other Nation, for Extent of Territory, the Pleasantness, Healthfulness, Fruitfulness thereof, and the good Disposition of the Inhabitants. The faithful and judicious *Portuguese* unknown Author of that Expedition, in a few Words thus describes this Province.

It consists of Hills and Vallies between. " Their Granaries were full of *Indian* Corn, " and other Edibles; so populous, that their " Towns and Fields, sow'd with Corn, " touch'd each other ; the Country is very " agreeable, by Reason of many Rivulets, " which make lovely Meadows. There grow " naturally in the Fields, Prunes, better " than we can in *Spain* produce by Cul- " ture, even in our Gardens. Vines mount, " in almost all Places near the Rivers, to " the Tops of the Trees. There are divers " other Sorts of Vines which are low, and " some run upon the Ground, and by cul- " tivating might be wonderfully improv'd, " tho' very good and pleasant, as they are " in their natural State. "

Below these on the same River, are the *Ullibalies*, or as some, the *Olibahalies* and according to the *French* the *Allibamous* : And below them the *Tallises*, who dwell upon a fair River which enters that of *Coza* from the East, thence to the once great Province of *Tasculuza*, almost destroy'd by *Ferdinando Soto* ; but the chief City *Mouvilla*, which
the

the *English* call *Maubela,* and the *French Mobile,* is yet in Being, tho' far fhort of its former Grandeur. About 100 Miles from hence, it enters the Gulph of *Mexico,* being firft increas'd, as by many fmall Rivers and Rivulets, fo by the fair River of the *Chattas,* which is made by a Colletion of feveral other little Streams and Rivers, and which at length form a fine River that would feem confiderable, if it were not obfcur'd by the great River in which it is loft. This mighty Nation of the *Chattas* confifting of near 3000 Fighting Men, live chiefly about the Middle of the River, and is not far from the *Chicaza's,* whom I mention'd to inhabit 30 or 40 Towns, in the Defcription of the *Cafqui* or *Cufates* River, and fpeak the fame Language. And to the Eaft between them and the *Cozas,* are the *Becaes* or *Abecaes,* who have 13 Towns, and dwell upon divers fmall Rivers, which run into the *Couffa.* It is a very pleafant Country, like that of the *Coza,* full of Hills and Vallies; their Ground is generally more marly, or fatter than many other Provinces; which are moftly of a lighter Mould. And a little more to the South-Weft, between the *Becaes* and *Chattas,* dwell in divers Towns, being 500 Fighting Men, the *Ewemalas,* upon a fair River of their Name, which coming from the Eaft, mixes with the *Couffa.* This mighty River enters the Gulph of *Mexico,* about 15 Leag. to the Weft of the great Bay of *Naffau* or
Spirito

Spirito Santo, or from the N. E. Cape of Mirtle Ifle, which is the South Land, between which, and the Continent to the North, is the Entrance of that vaft Inlet. The River runs into a Kind of a *Lagune* or Bay, which is barred 4 Miles from the Mouth of the River, fuppos'd to be occasion'd, as the *Mefchacebe,* in long Procefs of Time, by the Silt or Sediment of the Water, this being almoft as muddy, coming, for the moft Part, thro' a rich Clay or Marle; fo that at the Barr, when it is Low-Water (and it flows little there; excepting the South Wind drive in a great Sea) there is not above 14 or 15 Foot; but the Mouth being fome Miles Broad, and our People not having Leifure to examine nicely, perhaps there may be found deeper Places upon other Parts of the Barr; but fo foon as you are over it, there is a moft noble Harbour, very large, from 4 to 6 Fathom Depth. Near the Mouth of this River the *French* have lately made a new Settlement, call'd *Fort Louis,* which is the ufual Refidence of the Chief Governor of *Louiafiana,* who is neverthelefs fubordinate to him of *Canada.* In this Fort are fome Companies of Soldiers, and from thence Detachments are fent to fecure the feveral Stations, they have amongft the *Indians* in the Inland Parts.

As the *Ullibalys* or *Allibamous, Chicazas,* and *Chattaes,* are the moft populous and Potent Nations upon and between this River and the

the *Meschacebe*, the *English* for several Years
resided peaceably amongst, carry'd on a
considerable Trade with, and were as Friends
kindly entertain'd by them, till about the
Year 1715. by the Intrigues and Practices
of the *French*, they were either murther'd,
or oblig'd to retire, and make Room for
those new Intruders, who have since un-
justly possess'd and fortify'd the very same
Stations, in order to keep the Natives in
Awe and Subjection, and to cut off the
Communication of the *English* Traders with
the *Indians* thereabouts, and as far as, and
beyond the *Meschacebe*; whereby they have
secur'd to themselves an extensive and profitable Trade of above 500 Miles, which the
Subjects of *Great Britain* were a few Years
ago the Sole Masters of.

Besides the *French* Settlement abovemention'd on the Continent, they have another
small Town and Fort in the Isle *Dauphine*;
formerly call'd *Slaughter* Island, from a great
Number of Mens Bones found there on its
first Discovery, the Remains, as is said,
of a bloody Battle fought between two Nations of *Indians*. This Island lies about 9
Leag. South of *Fort Louis*, and 14 Leag.
West of *Pensacola*. It is inhabited and fortify'd only on Account of its Harbour, it
being the first Place the *French* Shipping
usually touch at in their Voyage from
France. The Distance between this River,
and that of *Palache* or *Spirito Santo* to the
East,

Eaſt, is about 190 Miles. The Coaſt between them is very deep and bold, contrary to all former Maps ; for thoſe ſent upon Diſcovery ſounded ſeveral Times every Day and found it ſo, as by the Journals will appear.

Between thoſe two great Rivers are divers Harbours, the Chief and indeed the beſt, upon all the Coaſt of the Gulph of *Mexico*, is *Penſicola*, a large Harbour, and very ſafe from all Winds, has 4 Fathom at the Entrance, and deepens gradually to 7 or 8. To the Eaſt of the Harbour, enters a fine River, which comes about 100 Miles out of the Country, and is made of two Rivers, which unite ſome Miles above. This Harbour or Bay lies 90 Leagues Weſt from the upper Part of the *Peniſula* of *Florida*. On the Lar-Board or Weſt-ſide of the Harbour ſtands a poor Town containing about 40 *Palmetto* Houſes, with a ſmall ſtockadoed Fort of 12 or 14 Guns, but of little Moment ; becauſe all their Soldiers, and the Majority of the Inhabitants, are *Forc'adoes* or forc'd People, having been Malefactors in ſome Parts of *Mexico*, therefore are confin'd in that Place for a Number of Years, according to the Nature of their Crimes. In ſhort they are not unlike our Felons, which are tranſported from the Jails in *England* to the Plantations. The *French* in the Year 1719. took this Fort with ſmall Loſs from the *Spaniards*, who in a few Months retook it again. The firſt of theſe made themſelves

Maſters

Masters thereof a second Time, but whether they have deserted it, or keep it still in
their Possession I know not.

If the *French* secure this Port and Harbour,
which is not above 14 Leagues East of their
chief Settlement at *Mobile*, they may with
ease, at all Seasons, infest, with large Men of
War and Privateers, the Navigation of the
English and *Spaniards* in the Bay of *Mexico*,
by lying in Wait for and intercepting their
Fleets and private Ships, trading to and
from *Panuco*, *Vera Cruz*, *Campeche*, *Porto Bel-
lo*, *Jamaica*, and the *Havana*.

Thirty Leagues to the East is *Apalatchy-
Cola*, which is also a good Harbor, and
West of *Apalatchy* River 30 Leagues.

The Bay of *Nassau* or *Spirito Santo* is made
by Four Islands, which run almost due South,
a little inclining to the West. The most
Northerly, between which and the Main is
the Entrance of the Bay, being 8 Leagues
long, our People call'd *Mirtle-Island*, from
the great Quantity of that Tree or Shrub,
which grows there, where digging they
found excellent good Water very plentifully.
This Island in some Places is very narrow.
Whether it be the same the *French* call *Isle
aux Vaisseaux*, or Ships Island, I can't tell,
but its Situation, Distance from *Isle Dauphine*,
or Slaughter Island, and its Commodiousness
for sheltring Ships from the Wind, creates a
Probability of its being so. The Bay is 15
Miles broad, from Mirtle Island to a Row
of

of Iſlands, which run Parallel with the Main,
and another Bay or *Lagune* between them,
within which They did not go. Theſe
Iſlands ſtretch Southward 50 or 60 Miles,
as far as one of the ſmaller Mouths of the
Meſchacebe, and doubtleſs there muſt be
very good Harbours, being defended from
the Sea and Winds by a double Row of
Iſlands, and having probably good Depths.
Our People viſited only the moſt Northerly,
which they nam'd Roſe-Iſland, a moſt fra-
grant Smell coming from it 3 Leagues off,
which exceeded all Perfumes; it is about
16 Miles long, and 2 Leagues or more from
the Northern or Weſtern Main. Between
this and *Mirtle-Iſland*, the Depths of Water were 4, 5, 6, 5, 4 Fathom. *Roſe-*
Iſland is a brave Iſland, and full of Wood.
They found it ſomewhat difficult to go
down the Bay between the Iſlands, meeting
with ſome Shoals, where they had not much
above 2 Fathom Water. They turn'd round
Mirtle-Iſland into the Main-Sea, and coaſted
the Eaſt-ſide, which is very bold. Over a-
gainſt *Mirtle-Iſland* to the North, about 5
Leagues diſtance, on the Main-Land, is a
high Point of Woods, where is the Entrance
of *Little Meſchacebe*, or the Eaſt Branch which
I mention'd in my Deſcription of the great
River. And about 15 Leagues to the North
Eaſt of this Branch of the *Meſchacebe*, is the
Bay of *Bilocchy*, which is, within a fair
Harbour, with a ſmall River falling into or
near

near it, call'd *Paſſagoula*, bordering on which
and the aforesaid Bay , is a fine Country,
but on the Barr there is not above 7 or 8
Foot Water. It was on the Continent lying, I think, on the Easterly Part of this
Bay, that Monſieur *d' Iberville* in the Beginning of the Year 1700. built a ſmall Sconce,
and left therein about Forty Men well provided with Neceſſaries. He afterwards return'd twice to *France* for further Reinforce-
ments, but on his Third Voyage back to
Bilocohi he died. The *French* being about
that Time hotly engag'd in a War with the
Engliſh and their Confederates in *Europe*, this
and another ſmall Settlement, they had thereabouts, were deſerted, for Want of timely
and neceſſary Supplies.

Our Ship paſs'd on the Eaſt-ſide of *Mirtle-
Iſland*, which is 24 Miles long, and Three
other Iſlands, there being Openings between
a Mile or 2 over. The Fourth and Laſt
Iſland, is the broadeſt and higheſt, and a
good Mark to find the *Meſchacebe*. Theſe
Iſlands lie all together in a direct Line South
and by Weſt, Eaſt and by North, at leaſt
50 Miles, and have all along, 2 Leagues off,
from 5 to 9 Fathom Water. When you
come to the Fourth Iſle you muſt be cau-
tious, the Sounding being uncertain ; for
ſome Points of Sand ſtretch out into the Sea
3 Leagues, and varies the Depths from 9
Fathoms to 4, then 8, 9, all at once. Between

tween this Island and the Main, is a Paſſage 2 Leagues broad, which leads into the
great Bay from which they came. The
Length of the Bay from North to South is
one entire Degree. They went divers Leagues up it, and found deep Water; but afterwards it Shoaling, they came down South,
and doubled the Cape, where the moſt Eaſterly of the Three great Branches of the *Meſchacebe* enter'd the Sea, which, with the Two
others to the Weſt, I deſcribed before, when
I gave an Account of the Mouths of that
River.

Altho' the Latitude and Longitude of the
Mouths of the *Meſchacebe* were perfectly
known, yet it is almoſt impoſſible, in the
Common Way of Sailing to come at them;
for if you go never ſo little to the South,
you will be driven by a very ſtrong Current to the South-Weſt 2 Miles an Hour,
till you come to the Bottom or Weſt-End
of the Gulph of *Mexico*; to prevent which
you muſt make the Main of *Florida* in about
30 Degrees of Latitude. The Land is ſo
very low you can ſcarcely ſee it, at 4
Leagues diſtance, where there is 45 and
50 Fathom, but 10 Leagues off, there's no
Ground at 100 Fathom. *Penſicola* is the moſt
convenient Place to fall in withall; and to
be ſure of that, your beſt Way is to make
the *Tortuga* Iſlands, which are Seven, and
but few Leagues diſtance to the N. W. from
the Cape of *Florida*, and the little Iſlands
which

which lie before it, call'd *Los Martyres*. The *Tortuga* Iſlands lie between the Latitude of 24 Degrees, and from 35 to 50 Minutes. They are not in a Round, as commonly repreſented in Charts, but bear almoſt N. and South. If you come there in the Months of *April*, *May*, or the Beginning of *June*, you will find great Numbers of Tur-tle, which are then in good Plight, extra-ordinary good Food both freſh and ſalted, and a wholſome Change of Diet for Sea-men, afterwards they will not well take Salt, decaying and running into a Gelly or Water , and before *July* is expir'd quite leave the Iſlands 'till the next Year. The Courſe from the *Tortuga* Iſlands to *Penſicola*, is N. 44 W. diſtance 158 Leagues, the Shore bold, bearing Eaſt and Weſt. Nine Leagues from the Land you will have 33 Fathom Water, but if you make the Ri-ver of the *Cozas* or *Couſſas* which is 167 Leagues, and a very remarkable Place, be-ing a ſpacious large Opening, having a ſmall ſandy Iſle in the Middle, you'll find the Land ſtretch Eaſt and Weſt, and within a-bout 18 Leagues you will fall in with *Mir-tle-Iſland*, which, with the Main, makes the Entrance into the great Bay of *Spirito Santo* ; in which Iſle, as I ſaid before, is very good freſh Water. This with Five or Six other low Iſles, run in a Range 14 Leagues, and S. W. from them, about 5 Leagues, are high Woods : Stand over for the South Part

D of

of thefe Woods, until you come to 4 Fathom, there caft your Anchor, and fend
your Boat to a low Point along the Shore
to the Southward. In 5 Foot Water you
will find a fmall Branch of the River; row
up it, the Current, will carry you to the
Barr, where you may take your Marks for
the Entrance into it. Perhaps fome Times
the Waters may be fo low that you cannot
pafs this Channel: In Cafe this fhould happen (which I fuppofe it feldom or never
doth) then run by the Soundings of the
Shore, in 5 or 6 Foot Water, and keep that
Depth till you come to the Pitch of the
Eaft Cape, where you will find the Eafterly
Branch in 14 or 15 Foot Water : Then row
up, take your Marks, return, and place two
Buoys, and you may carry your Ship in
to the River very fafely , as you may
perceive by the Draught. The fame or
like Caution muft be us'd, for entering into
either of the other Mouths, to keep near
the Shore, and by anchoring ftop the Tide
of Ebb. There is a Bay, which our Men
in the Ship, call'd *Salt-Water Bay* ; They
who went to the Head of it , *Frefh-
Water-Bay* ; a feeming Contradiction, but
thus eafily reconcil'd. This Bay lies between
the Eaft and Middle great Branch of the
River : The great Branches bring down fo
confiderable a Quantity of Water, at the
Ebb, with a ftrong Currrent, that then the
frefh Water enters the Sea 2 or 3 Leagues,
and

and between them the Sea enters this Bay,
not mixing with the Waters of the Rivers,
which are 10 Miles diſtant; ſo that Ships,
who anchor at the lower End of the Bay,
find the Waters Salt ; but there is a Creek,
at the N. W. End of the Bay, which comes
out of the Middle Branch, and a little before it enters the Bay is divided. This
Creek hath from 8 Foot at the ſhalloweſt
to 9, 10 and 11 Foot Water, by which
they enter'd, out of *Salt-Water Bay*, into
the River.

C H A P. III.

*A Deſcription of the Sea-Coaſt,
the large Rivers, their Heads
and Courſes, beyond or to the
Weſt of* Meſchacebe.

AVING made a faithful Narrative,
from good Journals and Itineraries by
Sea and Land, of the great River
Meſchacebe, the Rivers increaſing it, the
Countries adjacent, and Inhabitants thereof:
As alſo of the Countries, People, Rivers
and Harbors, towards the Eaſt belonging
unto this Province, which do not communi-

D 2   cate

cate with it, I shall give a brief Relation
of what I have learn'd, concerning the Sea
and Coast thereof, beyond the *Meschacebe*, to
the West, the Rivers belonging to this Province, their Heads and Courses, which enters not the *Meschacebe*.

When you are pass'd the Third or Westerly Branch of the *Meschacebe*, there presents
it'sself a fair Bay going to the North, into which empties themselves two of the
smaller Branches of the great River, as may
be discern'd in the Chart. This Bay is between 20 and 30 Miles deep, and very bold
to the East, having from the Entrance unto the Bottom, from 25 to 6 Fathom; but
is not in those Depths, above 7 or 8 Miles
broad, a Sand running from the Main 30
Miles South into the Sea, upon which there
is not above 3 Fathom, which yet our Ship
pass'd, going and returning. At the North
East End of the Bay, the great River runs
Parrellel with it for some Miles, from a
Mile to a Mile and a Half distance from it,
and two fair, large deep Creeks enter it,
almost in the Middle, out of the Westerly
great Branch of the River. Having pass'd
this Shoal to the Main, the Land runs almost
due East and West, having a bold Coast,
for a 100 Miles until you come to a great
Shoal, where there is not above 2 or 3 Fathom Water, with several Breakers. Our
People sail'd 62 Leag. on the S. side of this
great Shoal, always out of the sight of Land,
therefore

therefore knew not the Breadth : They kept
near the Latitude of 29 Degrees, the Depths
generally as follows, 7, 8, 9, 8, 7, 6 Fathom : At length they came to the Bottom of the Bay or Gulph, from whence they
return'd unto the Westerly Branch of the
Meschacebe.

From the River *Meschacebe* unto the Bottom of the Bay are innumerable fine small
Rivers, very pleasant : Great Store of Buffaloes or wild Kine frequent them to the
very Sea-side, as also Deer of divers Sorts,
wild Turkies, and many other large Water
and Sea-Fowl ; the Coast abounds with
good Fish ; but I cannot learn there are
above Four very large Rivers, and of long
Course.

The first and greatest is that of the *Quonoatinnos,* or of the *Coenis,* a great and populous Nation, who dwell in Forty or Fifty
Villages upon the Middle of this River, and
others which run into it. They are about
five Days Journey distant from the Habitations of the *Spaniards* and near 200 Miles
from the Sea, into which the River empties
itself, about 80 Leagues to the West of the
Meschacebe ; it is broad, deep, and Navigable almost to its Heads, which chiefly proceed from the Ridge of Hills that separate
this Province from *New Mexico :* And its
North West Branches, approach near the
South-West Branches of the River of the
Houmas. There dwell upon it, more towards

D 3

wards its Mouth, divers other Nations, whose Names are unknown, excepting the *Tarahas*, *Tycappans*, *Paloguessens* and *Palonnas*: All these Nations have good Horses.

About 30 Leagues further to the South of the West, is the River of the *Kirononas*, who with divers other Nations dwell there-upon. It is little less than that of the *Konoatinnos*, and as that hath its Sources in the Mountains of *New Mexico*, the Course of this is likewise from the N. W. until it enters the Sea.

Between this and the aforesaid River of *Quonoatinnos* or *Coenis*, lies the Bay of St. *Bernard*, call'd by Monsieur *de la Salle*, the Bay of St. *Louis*, and a River that falls into it he nam'd the River of *Vaches*. In the Year 1685. he built there a Fort (after he had purposely, as it is said, overshot the Mouth of the River *Meschacebe*) having form'd a Design from thence to visit the Mines of St. *Barbe* in *New Biscay*, which were not much, above 300 Miles distant. But one of his Vessels returning to *France*, and the other Three being lost with great Part of his Stores, Ammunition and Provisions; withal failing in his Attempt to engage the *Indians* in his Party and Interest, who, instead of Friends, prov'd his mortal Enemies, con-tinually sculking about his infant Settlement, and destroying many of his People, he was oblig'd to desist from that Enterprize. He afterwards with Twenty chosen Men went

by

by Land in search of the River *Meschacebe*, in which Attempt he lost his Life, being barbarously murther'd by some of his own Followers. This Fort was soon after taken and destroy'd by the *Spaniards* and *Indians*, all the *French* remaining therein, being either kill'd or made Prisoners.

About the same Distance further S. W. is the River of the *Biscaterongs*, which is of the same Magnitude with the former, hath the same Course from the N. W. to the Sea, and its Heads from the same Mountains.

The last River of Note is a River of much the same Bigness with the two preceding, and enters the Bay of *Mexico* at the N. W. End, between the Degrees of 27 and 28, it is nam'd *Abotas*.

It may not be amiss to mention another River, which altho' it be not within the Bounds of this Colony, may be of great Use, when it is well establish'd, by Reason of the Conveniency of Traffick with the *Spaniards*, it being near the aforesaid famous Mines of *New Biscay*, a large Province lying between *Mexico* and *New Mexico*. This stately River hath its Fountains, in the most Northerly Parts of *New Mexico* in the Latitude of 38 Degrees, and being gradually increas'd by the Conflux of many small Waters, becomes large and Navigable, till it approaches the 30th Degree; then it turns to the S. E. and enters a Parcel of high Mountains, from whence it is no fur-

D 4

ther

ther Navigable ; it is call'd by the *Spaniards*, *Rio Bravo.* They differ in their Accounts hereof; some affirming it is swallow'd up in a hideous Gulph, and passes Three Days Journey under the Earth, like their great River *Guadiana* in *Spain*, of which their famous Embassador *Gundamore* said, when asked, Whether his Master could shew such a Bridge as that over the *Thames* at *London*, that he had a Bridge upon which many Hundred Thousand Sheep daily fed. Others write that the River doth not dive under Ground , but passes among Rocks full of streight Passages, with many Cataracts; that after it has broke its Way through, it glides very placidly cross a level Country for a 150 Miles, being both large and deep, and at length empties itself into a broad and long *Lagune*, which is Navigable, with two or three Passages into it, between the Islands that form it, and whose Entrances are at least between 3 and 4 Fathom deep. I have a Journal of Captain *Parker*, who in the Year 1688, was there with Two Ships: One very large in search of a *Spanish* Wreck, but will not trouble my Reader with the Relation of what there happen'd to them. All Accounts agree this Country is well watered, that it abounds with vast Quantities of Wild Kine, the *Spaniards* call *Cibolas*, and is fruitful, pleasant and populous.

CHAP.

****

C H A P. IV.

A Description of the five great Seas or Lakes of fresh Water, which are to the North *of this Province, and the* West *and* North West *of our other Plantations, on the* East *Side of the River* Meschacebe, *with the Rivers falling into them, the Countries bordering thereon, and the several Nations of* Indians *who inhabit therein.*

I Think it not inexpedient to give an Account of the great Seas or Lakes of fresh Water, which are to the North of this Country, on the East side of the *Meschacebe*, which though not in the
Bounds

Bounds of this Province, may prove very beneficial, both to the Inhabitants of this and our Colonies of *New York*, *Penſilvania*, *Maryland*, and *Virginia*, who are not very remote from ſome of them, and may have an eaſy Acceſs thereunto, and conſequently by Navigation with thoſe that are more remote, they having all Communication with each other, as may be preſently diſcern'd by the Map.

The Seas or Lakes are Five. Firſt the ſuperior Lake beforemention'd, it being of almoſt Northerly, and is call'd by moſt of the Savages, the Lake of the *Nadoueſſons*, the greateſt and moſt valiant Nation of the North, divided into ſeveral Tribes, who go by divers Names. This Lake is eſteem'd at leaſt 150 Leagues in Length, 60 Leagues in Breadth, and 500 in Circumference. The South ſide, which we reckon its length is all along ſituated in very near 46 Dégrees of Latitude from the Eaſt End to the Weſt. The North ſide where it is broadeſt, is in about 49 Deg. It is all over Navigable, hath ſome Iſles; but one eſpecially call'd *Minong* above 60 Miles in Compaſs, wherein, both *Indians* and *French* affirm, is a great Mine of very pure Copper, which from the Oar, affords without any Preparation beſides melting, above 3 Fifths fine Metal. It is very remarkable of this Sea, that on all the South ſide upon the Shore, it is not above 4 or 5 Fathom deep, and gradually increaſes as you

you pass over to the North, until you cannot find Bottom with 150 Fathom of Line. It is most wonderfully stored with admirable Fish, and the Land about it with Deer and Elk, or Moose, especially the North side. With this latter and some Islands, the *French* drive a considerable Trade among the Natives, for Skins and Furrs; and of late Years have intercepted a great Part of the more remote *Indians*, who us'd formerly to Traffick with the *English*, in *Hudson's Bay*, at *Port Nelson* and *New Severn*. This Lake or Sea is made up of innumerable small Rivers and Rivulets, and Three large Rivers, all on the North side of the Lake, entering at the N. E. End thereof, whose Names are *Lemipiffaki*, *Michipiketon* and *Nemipigon*, which last proceeds out of a Lake, of the same Name, full of Islands; at the upper End whereof, enters a River, which comes from the North, and hath its Origine from divers small Lakes and Marshes. The Lake of *Nemipigon* is above 200 Miles in Compass. The *Barron le Hontan* is certainly mistaken about the Original of this River, and makes it vastly bigger than it is; he accounts it the Head of the great River of *Canada* or St. *Laurence*, and to come out of the Lake of the *Affenipouvals*; but I have been inform'd by a Person who liv'd two Years in those Parts, and had often been upon these two Lakes, that the Lake of the *Affinepoualaos* (for that is the true Name) which

is

is confiderable to the N. W. and as the *Indians* often affur'd, was the biggeft Lake in all this Northern Continent, had no Communication with that of *Nemipigon*. The N. W. of this Lake *Superiour* or of the *Nadoueffons*, is not above 30 Leagues in a ftreight Line ; from the Lake of *Nemipigon* ; but the Communication by Land is difficult , by Reafon the Earth abounds with Bogs and Marfhes.

The great or fuperior Lake empties itfelf into that of *Karegnondi* or the deep Lake , it being in moft Parts more profound than the Three we fhall hereafter mention. Formerly it was call'd the Lake *Hounondate*, from a great Nation, who inhabited on its Eaft fide, nam'd from their brifly Hair on their Head, *Hurons*, fince totally deftroy'd or difpers'd into very remote Parts by the *Irocois*.

This Lake is much of the Figure of an æquilateral Triangle, whofe Bafis is to the North. It abounds with divers Sorts of excellent Fifh, great and fmall, efpecially a large Fifh nam'd *Affihendo*, of the Bignefs of *Newfoundland* Codd. This Fifh is the *Manna* of moft of the Nations which inhabit about the Lake, being half their Subfiftance. And *Europeans* of all Nations, who have eaten thereof, agree, there is not in Seas or Rivers, a better tafted, more wholfome Fifh, and the Numbers are fuch as of Codd on the Bank of *Newfoundland*, and never to be leffen'd.

lessen'd. Besides these, there is Abundance
of good Sturgeons, Salmons or Salmon
Trouts, weighing from Twenty to Fifty
Pounds, large Carps, and many other Kinds
of Fish, small and great, not inferior to any
in *Europe*. The Inhabitants almost round
this Lake are mostly destroy'd by the *Irocois*, except a small Remnant of Two or
Three Nations, who have, with the Help of
the *French*, erected a strong Fort, near another built by that Nation for a Refuge to
their Allies and Traders, when the *Irocois*
happen to invade these, or the adjacent
Parts. This Lake hath many Islands, especially on the North side, where the greatest Fishery is for the *Assihendo*, but none at
Maintoualin, which is 20 Leagues long and
10 broad, lying directly over against the
Continent, from which it is only 6 or 7
Leagues distant.

The North-side of the Country bordering
upon this Lake, is not so pleasant in most
Places as the South, East and West; but
to make amends, it abounds with all Sorts
of Skins and Furrs, and hath these great
Conveniencies, that by the River of the
Nepiserini, there is a Communication with
all the *French* of *Canada*, and many Nations bordering thereupon; for ascending this
River, you enter into a large Lake of the
same Name, which is made by divers small,
and one large River coming far from the
North-West. Near this Lake, passes the
great

gret River of the *Outouacks*, once a great
Nation, but now almoſt extirpated by the
aforeſaid *Irocois*, which after a Courſe of
100 Leag. brings you to the Iſland and City
of *Montreall*, the next for Bigneſs and
Strength to *Quebec*, the Capital of *Canada*,
and there joins with the great River of St.
Laurence; from the Juncture of thoſe Two
Rivers to *Quebec*, is 60 Leagues. Both Sides
of the River are inhabited all the Way in
Plantations very little remote from each
other; beſides Two or Three ſmall Towns
and Fortifications. Such another Communication there is, though much more eaſy,
of which I ſhall diſcourſe at large, when
I come to deſcribe the lovely *Peninſula* of
Erie.

Towards the lower End of the South-
Weſt Continent, is the large and fair Bay
of *Sakinam*, which is about Fifty Miles
deep and 18 wide, and in the Middle of
the Opening are Two Iſles very advan-
tageouſly ſituated, for ſheltring Boats or o-
ther Veſſels, that happen to be ſurpriz'd
with a Storm; there being no other Harbour within divers Leagues. Into the Bottom
of this Bay empties itſelf, after a Courſe of 60
Leagues, a very ſtill quiet Stream, excepting
Three ſmall Falls, paſs'd eaſily and without
the leaſt Danger. On this River and the
Branches thereof, is one of the greateſt
Beavour Huntings in *America*. Twenty
Leagues from this Bay to the South-Eaſt,
this

this Lake, which is above 400 Leagues in
Circumference, empties itself into the Lake
Erie by a Channel, which I shall describe,
when I have given an Account of the Lake
of the *Illinouecks*, which is to the West of
Karegnondi, and communicates therewith,
towards the N. W. End, by a Streight, 9
or 10 Miles long, and 3 or 4 broad. The
Breadth of it on the North Coast, is 40
Leag. but it increases gradually in Breadth,
till you come to the Bottom of the Bay.
The North-side is in the Latitude of 45
and 30 Minutes; the South in almost 42
Degrees. Forty Leagues from the Entrance
due West, it makes the great Bay of the
Poutouotamis, a Nation who inhabit a large
Country upon, and to the South of this
Bay, which is 8 Leagues broad, and 30
Leagues deep, South and by West, the Entrance being full of Islands. And into the
Bottom comes the fair River *Miscouaqui*, after a Course of 200 Miles. This River is
remarkable upon divers Accounts : First
when you are ascended it 50 Leagues, there
is a Carriage of a little above a League
and a half; afterwards you meet with the
lovely River *Mesconsing*, which carries you
down into the *Meschacebe*, as I before declar'd. Next upon this River especially near
the Carriage, is a Country famous for *Bea-*
vour Hunting like that of *Sakinam.* You
must know, that most Parts of *North-Ame-*
rica have *Beavours* ; you shall scarce meet
with

with a Lake, where there are not some of
their Dams and Hutts. But these two Places
I have mention'd, and others I shall speak
of hereafter, are Countries 40 or 50 Miles
long, abounding with small Rivers and Rivulets, wherewith they make their Dams or
Cawsways ; and consequently small Lakes,
seated opportunely for Wood to build, and,
produces plentifully such Plants and young
Trees, upon which they mostly subsist. This
is chiefly possess'd by the industrious and valiant Nation of the *Outogamis*. Thirdly, This
River and others entering thereinto, abound
in that Corn call'd *Malomin*, which grows
in the Water in marshy wet Places, as Rice
in the *Indies*, *Turkey* and *Carolina*, &c: But
much more like our Oats, only longer, bigger, and better, than either that, or *Indian*
Corn, and is the chief Food of many Nations hereabouts and elsewhere. The Nations who dwell on this River, are *Outoga-
mis*, *Malominis*, *Nikic*, *Oualeanicou*, *Sacky*, and
the *Poutouatamis* beforemention'd.

On the East-side of this Lake, about 20
Leagues from the Streight by which it enters *Karegnondi*, is a Bay call'd *Bear Bay*,
and a River of the same Name, because of
great Numbers of those Animals, who haunt
those Parts. This River comes out of a
Ridge of Hills near 100 Leagues long, beginning almost at the North End of this
Peninsula, out of which flow abundance
of small Rivers; those, whose Course is to
the

the Eaſt, empty themſelves into the Lake *Karegnondi*. Thoſe to the Weſt, into that of the *Alinouecks*. The Top of this Ridge of Hills is flat, from whence there is a delicious Proſpect into both Lakes , and level as a Taraſſe-Walk. There is a great *Beaver* Hunting, like thoſe I formerly mention'd, upon *Bear River*, which hath a Courſe of 40 or 50 Leagues. On the Weſt-ſide of the Lake, before you come to the Bottom, is a Harbour capable of ſmall Ships ; and there enters into it a ſmall River, which at 2 Leagues diſtance, approaches the River *Checagou*, the North Branch of the River of the *Allinouecks*, which is, from the main Branch of the ſaid River 50 Miles. Near the Bottom of the Bay on the Eaſt-ſide, is the fair River of the *Miamihas* (ſo call'd becauſe upon it lives Part of a Nation bearing the ſame Name) which in its Paſſage comes within 2 Leagues of the great Eaſterly Branch of the River of the *Allinouecks*, and its Springs are very near the Heads of ſome Rivers which enter the *Ouabachi*. Monſieur *de la Salle* on his firſt Arrival in this River, which was about the Year 1679. finding it admirably well ſituated for Trade, and the Country ſurrounding it extremely pleaſant and fertil, artfully gain'd the Permiſſion of the Natives to build a Fort therein, under the ſpecious Pretence of protecting them from the Inſults of the *Engliſh* and *Irocois*, whom he repreſented as cruel and

E   treache-

treacherous Enemies, continually plotting the Destruction of them, and all the *Indians* round about. In this Fort was formerly a great Magazine and Storehouse for all Sorts of *European* Goods, and hither the Traders and Savages continually resorted to purchase them. It commanded the Entrance into the Lake, and kept all the Neighbouring *Indians* in Awe and Subjection. Nations to the West of this Lake, besides the beforementioned, are Part of the *Outogamis, Mascoutens* and *Kikpouz*; then the *Ainoves*, the *Cascaschia*, and a little to the South-West of the Bottom of this Lake, and more to the North, the *Anthontans*, and Part of the *Mascoutens*, near the River *Misconsing*. The Countries surrounding this Lake, especially towards the South, are very charming to the Eye, the Meadows, Fruit-Trees and Forrests, together with the Fowls, wild Beasts, *&c.* affording most Things necessary for the Support and Comfort of Life, besides *Indian* Corn, with which the Natives abound; and *European* Fruits, Grains, and all other useful Vegetables, by Reason of the Goodness of the Soil, and Mildness of the Climate, would certainly thrive there, as well as in their Native Countries. But above all, the South Parts of the Countries bordering on this Lake, seem naturally dispos'd to produce admirable Vines, which being duly cultivated, excellent Wines might be made of the Fruits thereof, they growing naturally

in

in vaft Numbers of divers Sorts, fome ramping up to the Tops of the higheft Trees ;
others running upon the Ground : The
Grapes are fome very fmall, others wonderfully large, big as Damfons, and many of
a Middle Size, of divers Colours and Taftes ;
they are all good to eat, only fome, which
otherwife promife very well , have great
Stones or Kernels and tough Skins, which
certainly would be remedied by due Culture. But of the worft doubtlefs good
Brandy might be made, were there Artifts
and convenient Veffels for preffing, ferment-
ing and diftilling.

There ramble about in great Herds, e-
fpecially about the Bottom of this Lake, in-
finite Quantities of Wild Kine. Some Hundreds ufually together, which is a great
Part of the Subfiftance of the Savages who
live upon them while the Seafon of Huntt-
ing lafts ; for at thofe Times they leave
their Towns quite empty. They have a
Way of preferving their Flefh without Salt
6 or 8 Months, which both looks, and eats fo
frefh, Strangers apprehended the Cattle had
not been kill'd one Week. Befides, they
ufe the Hair, or rather Wool, cut off their
Hides, for Garments, and Beds, and fpin it
into Yarn, of which they make great Bags,
wherein they put the Flefh they kill, after
they have cured it, to bring Home to their
Houfes ; for their Huntings are from the
latter End of *Autumn*, when the Cattle are

fat,

fat, to the beginning of the Spring, and of the Hides dress'd they make Shoes *Ala Savage.*

But its Time we should return to the Lake *Keregnondi,* which empties itself into the Lake *Erie,* by a Channel 30 Leagues long, and where narrowest a League broad; in the Middle whereof is a small Lake, called by the *Indians, Otseka,* 10 Leag. long and 7 or 8 over, being of an Oval Figure. In this Lake and Channel, are divers small Islands, exceedingly pleasant and fruitful, in which, and all the Country, on both Sides of them, are great Quantities of Beasts and Fowl, as Deer of several Kinds, wild Turkies, Pheasants, and a large excellent Fowl, which they call *Dindo's.* The Lake *Erie* is about 250 Leagues long, and almost equally 40 broad. Eight Leagues from its Mouth are Eight or Ten Islands, most of them small; One in the Middle is 5 or 6 Miles in Circumference, and all very agreeable. Near the Mouth on the West-side, is a large Harbour for Ships, defended from most Winds, made like our Downs by a great Bank of Sand; tho' Winds seldom infest this Lake, in Respect of the others; where sometimes they Rage as in the Main Ocean, so that it may be deservedly call'd the Pacifick Lake. And if we may give Credit to the Relations of the *English* who have long frequented it, and unanimously agree herein, there is not a more pleasant Lake, or Country surrounding

rounding it in the Univerſe. It is not indeed ſo deep as the others, yet is in all
Places Navigable by the greateſt Ships, there
being ſeldom leſs then 10 or 12 Fathom
Water. The Land round about it is perfectly level, abounding with Trees, both
for Timber and Fruit, ſo happily plac'd that
One would be apt to apprehend it to be a
Work of great Art, and contriv'd to declare
the Grandeur and Magnificence of ſome
mighty Emperor, and not of Nature. Abundance of ſmall pretty Rivers, diſcharge themſelves thereinto, amongſt which are Four very
conſiderable and remarkable. One about 10
Leagues from the Entrance of the Canal, in
the Bottom of the Weſt End of the Lake,
that hath a Courſe of 60 Leagues, and its
Head very near the River of the *Miamihas*,
which runs into the S. E. Side of the Lake of
the *Illinouecks*, by Means whereof there is a
ſhort and eaſy Communication therewith,
which by Water is above 600 Miles.

Fifty Miles further to the South, at the
ſame Weſt End of this Lake, is another River much of the ſame Bigneſs and Length;
and about and between theſe two Rivers,
every Year in the Seaſon, are Multitudes of
the wild Kine call'd *Cibolas*.

At the S. E. End of the Lake there is a
Third River which has its Riſe very near
the great *Suſquehannah* River, which waters
Part of *Penſilvania*, and afterwards empties
itſelf into the North-End of the Bay of

Cheſe-

Chesepeak in *Maryland*. And 20 Leagues S. Westerly is another fair River which comes near 50 Leagues out of the Country; from whose Head, which issues from a Lake, is but a short Cutt to the River *Hohio*, from whence to a Branch of the aforesaid *Susquehannah* River is about 1 League.

By these two last mention'd Rivers, the *English* may have a ready and easy Communication with this and consequently with all the other Lakes. If the *French* should ever settle thereon, which for above Twenty Years they have endeavoured, but have been, in great Measure, wonderfully frustrated by the *Iroccis* our Subjects or Allies, they might greatly molest, by themselves and their *Indians*, the Colonies of *New-York*, *Pensilvania*, *Maryland* and *Virginia*, which, I hope by the Wisdom and Care of His Majesty and Ministry, will be speedily prevented.

At the North-East End of this Lake is another Canal 40 Miles long, and in most Places a League broad, call'd by the Natives *Niagara*, having a delicate level, beautiful, fertil Country on each Side of it; but being pass'd about two Thirds of the Way, it is straiten'd by mighty Rocks, and precipitates itself several Hundred Feet, being the greatest Catarack, that hath ever yet come unto our Knowledge, in the whole World. This lying within five or six Days Journey of *Albany* and *Schenecteda*, (two remarkable Towns and Fortifications of *New-York*)

York) and adjacent unto our Confederates
or Subjects the five Nations, (by the *French*
call'd *Irocois*) especially the *Sonnontovans* (by
some nam'd *Senecaes*) the most populous of
the Five. I have receiv'd an Account from
divers Persons, who have with great Attention and Curiosity view'd it, suiting very
well with the Description *Hennepin* gives
thereof, who had been there several Times.
The Noise of such a Multitude of Waters
falling from so great a Height, is so extraordinary, that altho' the Country is very
pleasant, level and fruitful below the Fall,
yet the *Sonnontovans* were not able to bear
it, but were forc'd to remove and settle 2
Leagues lower. I have had it from very credible People, that when the Wind sets due
South, they have heard it distinctly above
30 Miles. The River, as may be easily
imagin'd, below this Cataract, is very rapid,
for the Space of 3 or 4 Miles; then for 6
or 8, is more placid and navigable, until
it enters the Lake *Ontario*, which is 80
Leagues long, and in the Middle 25 or 30
broad, being of an Oval Figure. The Name
of this Lake in the *Irocois* Language (that
Nation bordering upon it to the South)
signifies the pleasant or beautiful Lake, as it
may be deservedly stil'd; the Country round
it being very champain, fertil, and every
2 or 3 Miles water'd with fine Rivulets: It
has on the South-side three fair Rivers;
that next the Fall coming out of the Coun-

try

try of the *Sonnontovans*, the Middle one
from the *Onontages*, and its Origin from a
Lake, within a League of their Capital
Town *Onontague*, made up of many little
Rivers and Rivulets, being 40 Miles in
Circumference, abounding with Fish of divers Sorts with some Salt-springs entring
into it. After the River hath pass'd a Mile
from the Lake, it receives another coming
from the West out of the Province of the
Onioets, who are Neighbours to the *Sonnon-*
tovans, in whose Country the Head of this
River springs. About 10 Miles lower it is
increas'd by a fair deep River, which comes
from the East, out of the Country of the
Oneiouks, one of the five Nations, situated
between the *Onontages* and the *Mohacks*, who
dwell in Three Towns on a fair River,
which runs, after a Course of 100 Miles,
into *Hudson*'s River near *Albany*. The River of the *Onontagues*, enters the Lake *On-*
tario 50 Miles from the little Lake whence
it derives its Origin.

Twenty Leagues to the East, is another
River somewhat less, but Navigable by
Sloops, and large Boats a considerable Way
into the Country.

About the same Distance likewise to the
East, the Lake forms a great River, which
the *French* call the River of the *Irocois*; but
the Natives *Kanadari*, which for the Space
of 60 Miles is very broad, full of fine
Islands, and runs quietly; then is interrupted

ed in its Courſe by divers Falls ſucceſſively; ſome very deep and long, for above
100 Miles, until it meets with the great
River of the *Outouacks*, at the End of the
Iſland and City of *Montreal*, and together
with that makes the River of *Canada* or St.
Laurence, ſo nam'd by the *French*, becauſe
diſcover'd on the Day dedicated to his Memorial.

The North-part of the Lake *Ontario* was
formerly poſſeſs'd by Two Tribes of the
Irocois, who were in Time of perfect Peace,
without the leaſt Provocation, but only to
get their Country, deſtroy'd, enſlav'd, or
ſent to *France*, and put into the Gallies;
of which you may read at large in the
Journals of the *Baron la Hontan*, an impartial and judicious Author, who ſaw and
relates that Tragedy with much Indigna-
tion.

The Nation of the *Irocois*, as they are
call'd by the *French*, for what Reaſon I
could never learn, who inhabit the South-
part of the Country are ſtil'd by the *Engliſh*, the five Nations, being ſo many, di-
ſtinct in Name, and Habitations, from each
other; But leagu'd by a moſt ſtrict Confederacy, like the Cantons of *Switzerland*,
which they frequently in a very ſolemn
manner renew; Eſpecially ſince the *French*
grew powerful in their Neighbourhood.
They have always been an excellent and
uſeful Barrier between us and them, being
ready

ready, on all Occasions, upon the most
slender Invitations, and the least Assistance,
to molest and invade them, unto whom,
they are the most irreconcileable Enemies,
and I think upon good Grounds ; although
the *French* say the hardest Things imaginable
against them ; but I believe unto any impartial Judges, they will appear more blame-
able themselves. The Original of this Enmity proceeded from the *French*, who, about
100 Years since, settled at the Place, now
their Capital, call'd *Quebeck*. The *Irocois*
knowing of the *French* little Habitation
(where were not above Forty Men) came
according to their usual Manner, being a-
bout 200 of their prime Youth, under an
esteem'd Captain to war against the *Algon-
quins*, then a very populous Nation ; and
to shew their Contempt of them, made
a Fort on the South-side of the River,
before they who dwelt on the North-side
could gather into a Body, Their Habitations or Villages being somewhat remote
from each other : But having drawn their
Forces together in great Numbers, they attack'd the *Irocois*, who always valiantly repuls'd them, with great Losses to their E-
nemies and little unto themselves. Whereupon the *Algonkins* had recourse unto the
French, desiring they would assist them with
their Thunder and Lightning darting En-
gines. They readily comply'd, and did
such Execution with their Guns, (which being

ing altogether new and very furprizing or rather aftonifhing) that the *Irocois* were difcomfited, not above Two or Three efcaping to give an Account thereof to their ownCountrymen, who by Tradition have propagated the Story to Pofterity ; which may, in fome Meafure, excufe the irreconcileable Enmity, this Nation hath conceiv'd againft the *French*, between whom there have been formerly almoft conftant Wars, accompanied with various Events : The *French* with their Allies endeavouring to extirpate them, who have hitherto bravely defended themfelves ; the *Englifh* for their Furrs fupplying them with Ammunition, and during Time of War with the *French*, powerfully affifting them. They have been a very ufeful Barrier, and without their help *New-York*, and probably other Neighbouring Provinces, had long fince been poffefs'd by the *French*, having been very flenderly aided from *England*.

The *French* in all their Writings concerning *Canada*, make many tragical Relations of, and Exclamations againft the barbarous Cruelties of this Nation exercis'd upon them, and the *Indians* their Allies ; but feldom tell us that the very fame Things are practic'd by themfelves and their *Indians* againft the *Irocois*, and often during Time of Peace : For when the *Irocois* or five Nations, as we call them, were abandon'd by Order of King *Charles* II. towards the latter End of his Reign, and during the whole Reign of K.

James,

James, and obnoxious unto the Resentments of the *French*, (The *English* being strictly forbidden any ways to assist them) They were under a Necessity of making a very disadvantageous Peace, which how perfidiously it was broken, may be seen at large in that faithful and judicious History of the *Baron la Hontan*. And had it not been for the Revolution in *England*, the *Irocois* had been totally destroy'd, or subjected unto the *French*, which, as I hinted before in the Preface, would have been of dreadful Consequence to divers of our *English* Colonies, on the Continent. 'Tis true, the *Irocois* have extirpated or subjected several Nations of *Indians* round about them; but it hath been either because they were in Confederacy with their Enemies, destroyed their Country, murther'd their People, hinder'd them in their *Beaver* Hunting (without which they could not subsist) or furnish'd their Enemies with Furrs, which occasion'd the increasing the Numbers of the *French* from *France*, and consequently threatned them with utter Ruin, when *Canada* shall be more populated from *Europe*. So that certainly the Measures they take for their own Preservation and Security, are more innocent, and excusable, than those have been by the *French*; Forty Years last past, exercis'd in *Europe*, whose Wars have according to a modest Calculation, occasion'd the Death of above Two Millions of their own Country People, and other *Europeans*,

ropeans, and moſt unjuſtly invaded or grie-
vouſly oppreſs'd their Neighbours ; Deſire
of increaſing their Wealth, enlarging their
Territories, or advancing the Glory of their
Great Monarch, being the chief Cauſes, tho'
ſome other ſlender and eaſily confuted Pretences, have ſometimes been alledg'd.

But to return unto the *Irocois* whom we call
Subjeĉts of the Crown of *England*, they only
ſtile themſelves Brethren, Friends, Allies,
being a People highly tenacious of their Liberty, and very impatient of the leaſt In-
croachments thereon. Theſe five Cantons
or Nations, have ſold, given, and in a
very formal Publick manner, made over
and convey'd to the *Engliſh* divers large
Countries conquer'd from the *Indians*, upon
the South-ſide of the great Lakes, as far as
the *Meſchacebe*, and the noble, beautiful,
fertil *Peninſula* ſituated between the Three
Middle Lakes : That of the *Hurons* to the
Weſt, *Ontario* to the Eaſt, and *Erie* to the
South ; a Country almoſt as large as *England* without *Wales* ; admirably ſeated for
Traffick, pleaſant, healthful, and fertil, as
any Part of *North-America* ; and the Territory to the South` is of the ſame Nature,
and Confines with the Borders of our Province of *Carolina*, which extends to all the
North-ſide of the Gulph of *Mexico*.

C H A P.

C H A P. V.

*A New and Curious Disco-
covery and Relation of an
eafy Communication betwixt
the River* Mefchacebe *and
the* South-Sea, *which feparates* America *from* China,
*by Means of feveral large
Rivers and Lakes, with a
Defcription of the Coaft of
the faid Sea to the Streights
of* Uries. *As alfo of a rich
and confiderable Trade to be
carried on from thence to*
Japan, China *and* Tartary.

I T will be one great Conveniency of
this Country, if ever it comes to be
fettled, that there is an eafy Communication therewith, and the *South-Sea*,
which

which lies between *America* and *China*, and
that two Ways : By the North Branch of
the great Yellow River, by the Natives
call'd the River of the *Maſſorites*, which
hath a Courſe of 500 Miles, Navigable to
its Heads or Springs, and which proceeds
from a Ridge of Hills ſomewhat North of
New Mexico, paſſable by Horſe, Foot, or Wag-
gon in leſs than half a Day. On the other
Side are Rivers, which run into a great
Lake, that empties itſelf by another great
Navigable River into the *South-Sea*. The
ſame may be ſaid of the River *Meſchaouay*,
up which our People have been, but not
ſo far as the *Baron le Hontan*, who paſs'd on
it above 300 Miles almoſt due Weſt, and
declares it comes from the ſame Ridge of
Hills abovemention'd ; and that divers Rivers from the other ſide ſoon make a large
River, which enters into a vaſt Lake, on
which inhabit Two or Three great Nations, much more populous and civiliz'd than
other *Indians* ; and out of that Lake a great
River diſimbogues into the *South-Sea*, which
is doubtleſs the ſame with that beforemention'd, the Head of the Two Rivers being
little diſtant from each other.

About Twelve or Fourteen Years ſince, I
had imparted unto me a Journal from a
Gentleman admirably well skill'd in Geo-
graphy, eſpecially of *America*, who had made
thither divers Voyages from *New England* ,
and all our *Engliſh* Plantations in *America*,
and

and vifited moft Parts of the Gulph of *Mexi-co*, where he became acquainted with one Captain *Coxton* a famous Privateer , who was towards the latter End of the Reign of King *Charles* II. entertain'd in His Maje-fty's Service : But whether he was difoblig-ed, or that his Genius prompted him to follow his old Trade, having with his Co-partners fitted up a Ship of Twenty-fix Guns , He failed to the *South-Sea*, with a Defign to take the Ship, which comes an-nually from the *Manillas* or *Philippine* Iflands in the *Eaft-Indies* to *Acapulco*, the Chief Port of *Mexico*; which Ship, as he had been well inform'd , ufually made that Part of the Continent, that lies between *Japan* and *Ame-rica*, at a famous Port in 42 Degrees. But when he came to the Head of the Ifland, or *Peninfula* of *California* (it being too foon by fome Months for the putting in Execu-tion his intended Defign,) romaging the Coaft, he difcover'd a great River in about Degrees North-Latitude, which enter'd a great Lake, near the Mouth whereof he found a very convenient Ifland, where he ftaid Two or Three Months to refit himfelf, happening to have a Man on board, who underftood the Language of the Country. The Natives finding he was engag'd in an Expedition againft the *Spaniards*, treated him very kindly, fupply'd him very chear-fully with whatfoever he wanted, and he contracted great Friendfhip with them. He

calls

calls them the Nation of *Thoya*. The *Spaniards*, as I find in divers of their Expeditions, call it *Thoyago*, sometimes *Tejago*. They are often at War with the *Spaniards*, who have been always repuls'd by them. They bring Thirty or Forty Thousand Men in one Body into the Field. These and Two other Nations Neighbouring, and not much inferior unto them, are accounted the most sensible and civiliz'd *Indians* in *America*.

When the Season came fit for their Expedition, they sailed West and by South, and happen'd to stop upon some Occasion at an Island call'd *Earinda* or *Carinda*, there were Five in all near each other, like the *Canary* Islands, but lay rounder, and were one with another about 50 or 60 Miles in Compass. The Inhabitants were not shy of them, but supply'd them with Provisions, and brought them Gold to barter for such Commodities of ours as they lik'd, and in Three or Four Days they purchas'd 86 *l*. Weight of that Metal. The Natives told them they were sorry they had no more, they taking Care to provide only against a certain Time of the Year for Persons, who came from the Sun-setting at a particular Season and barter'd divers Commodities with them for Gold. These Traders or Merchants must certainly be Inhabitants of *Japan*, which I gather from a large Relation in the History of that Island, publish'd by the *Dutch*, and translated into our Tongue, and makes the

F   Sixth

Sixth Volume of *Ogleby*'s Collections. They therein declare, That they sent from *Batavia* Two Ships (as they pretended) to discover a Passage from the North-East Part of *Japan*, round *Tartary* to *Europe*; Though, its very probable, they had other Views. These Ships were separated a little East of *Japan* by a Storm; the *Castrilome* proceeded, and found the Streight entring into the Gulph of *Tartary* or *Jesso*, and search'd the Coast on the West-side to 49 Degrees; the other Ship the *Blefkins* having suffer'd much by the Storm, put into the Port of *Namboe*; near the N. E. End of *Japan*, not doubting they should be kindly receiv'd, being in League, and having a Free Trade with that Empire; but while they were refitting, they were unexpectedly surpriz'd by the *Japanese*, sent to Court, and very strictly examin'd, whither they had not been at, or went not to discover the Gold Islands (as they call'd them) to the East, of which Traffick the Emperor is so jealous, that it is Capital for any to go thither except by his Permission, or to declare to others the Distance and Situation thereof; and had not the *Dutch* given uncontroulable Evidence, that they had not been, nor were they going thither, but only upon the forementioned Discovery, they had been all executed.

There are upon the Coast between *America* and *Japan* divers very large and safe Har-

Harbours, and a very good Climate, the
Coaſt ſtretching South-Weſt, moſtly from
40 to   Degrees of North-Latitude. The
Seas abound with Fiſh, and the Land with
Fowl and Veniſon. The Inhabitants are ſo-
ciable and hoſpitable. I have a Draught
and Journals of all the Coaſt from *America*,
with thoſe of divers Harbours, until you
are within about 100 Leag. of the Streight
of *Uries*, which the *Dutch* diſcover'd about
Sixty or Seventy Years ſince, and which is
the Entrance of the Sea or Gulph of *Tartary*,
lying 120 Leagues North-Eaſt from *Namboe*,
the moſt Northerly Haven and Promontory
of *Japan*. This Streight, or rather, theſe
Streights (there being Two made by a long
Iſland) are the Inlets into a great Sea or
Bay, into which diſimbogues a vaſt River,
on the Weſt-ſide of it, between 49 and 50
Degrees of North-Latitude, Navigable many Hundred Miles by the biggeſt Ships, and
is made by the Conflux of divers great Rivers, ſome of which come from the South-
Weſt, as *Chingola*, *Hilura*, *Ola*, *Sungoro*, and
their Fountains, near the great Wall of *China*, and run through the Dominions of the
Eaſtern *Tartars*, who are now Maſters of
China. Other Rivers from the North-Weſt,
proceed from the Territories of the *Czar* of
Muſcovy, who hath built divers large and
well fortify'd Cities on the Main River of
Yamour, and ſeveral of its Branches, as *Ne-
govim*, *Nepehou*, *Albazin*, *Argun*, *Nettinskoy*, &c.

This

This River of *Yamour* or *Amura*, hath a Course, from its furtheft Fountains, above 1200 Miles, without any Interruption by Cataracts fo frequent in all the other great Rivers in *Mufcovy*, as the *Oby*, *Jeniffeg* or *Jenifca*, &c. By this River you may Trade with the Inhabitants of *Jedfo* for Furrs, who have great ftore, and thofe very rich. They inhabit all the Coaft on both Sides the Mouth of the River, and a confiderable Way up it. You may likewife Traffick with the *Mufcovites* for the fame Commodities, who fell them there for a Fourth Part of what they yeild in *Mufcow* or *Archangel*; thefe Parts being above 4000 Miles almoft due Eaft, from *Mufcow* their Capital City, a moft prodigious, tedious and difficult Journey, as appears by divers large and accurate Journals, which have been many Years publifh'd in Print. And by means of the Rivers which come from the South-Weft, you may correfpond with the *Eaftern Tartars*, *Chinefe*, and the great rich Kingdom of *Tanguth*, all now united under one and the fame Emperor, being very civiliz'd Nations, and kind to Strangers. To fay nothing of the great and rich *Peninfula* of *Corea*, which is contiguous to one or two Branches of this River, was once a Province of *China*, hath the fame Manners and Language, and is now Tributary to the prefent Emperour. This River and its Branches are in a good Clime, it never varying

rying

rying above 2 or 3 Degrees from a due Easterly Course. Three or more Ships may be sent every Year , who may Part at the Streights of the *Tartarian* Gulph or Sea; one for *Tedzo* and the River; another for *Japan,* and a Third for *North China* to the great City *Tunxo,* the Port of *Pekin,* the Capital of that Kingdom, from which it is not above One Days Journey by Land or Water. And there is not a better Commodity, or of which more Profit may be made, than of the Furrs, which are so easily procur'd, and so soon brought unto that Imperial City, where, in the Court and among the Grandees, there is a prodigious Consumption of them, and most extravagant Prices given for them, especially those of the better Sort, tho' even the meanest come to an extraordinary good Market.

Thus, after a thorough Search and Discovery both by Sea and Land, have I given the Reader a Topographical Description of a Country, the timely Possession and due Improvement whereof by the *English* may be more beneficial to them, than all the other Colonies they are at present possess'd of : Besides that they will thereby secure forever all the rest of our Plantations upon the Continent of *America,* which if this Country be by them neglected , and suffer'd to remain in the Hands of any ambitious, Politick and powerful Prince or Potentate, may be distress'd, conquer'd or utterly exterminated.   C H A P.

✶✶✶✶✶✶✶✶✶✶✶✶✶✶✶✶✶✶✶✶✶✶✶✶✶✶✶✶✶✶✶✶✶

CHAP. VI.

An Account of the useful Animals, Vegetables, Mettals, Minerals, and other rich and valuable Commodities which are naturally produced or may with Industry be rais'd in this Province.

IN a new Colony the first Care is to provide Food for their Subsistance. The great Duke of *Rhoan* famous for Wisdom and Valour, who hath written so many celebrated Treatises, especially relating to Military Affairs, and Politicks, advances it as a Maxim, That he who will be a great Warrior, must in the first Place make Provision for the Belly ; and in the late War with the *French*, our seasonable and plentiful Supplies of the Soldiers hath not a little contributed to our wonderful Successes, and

and both ftrengthned and animated our Troops, to perform fuch Acts of Valour, as will be celebrated in Future Ages. The *Spaniards* tell a pretty, and I think inftructive Story, That upon the Difcovery of the immenfe Riches contain'd in the Mountain *Potofi* in *Peru*, two *Spaniards* reforted thither; the one bought Slaves, hir'd Servants, Overfeers, and found a rich Vein of Silver Oar. The other (Land being then Common in the Neighbourhood) fed Sheep. The Mine Mafter wanting Wool for the cloathing of his Servants (that Place being much colder than others in the fame Latitude) and Food for his Overfeers (who could not be fatisfied, being *Spaniards*, with the poor Fare of the *Indians* and *Negroes*) bought Flefh and Wool of the Shepherd, and after fome few Years the Shepherd grew rich, and the Mafter-Miner poor. If the *Spaniards* had further improv'd this Notion, the *Englifh*, *Dutch* and *French*, had not exchang'd fo many of their Manufactures for Gold and Silver; fo that they are the richeft and pooreft Nation in the Southern Part of *Europe*.

And even our own Nation hath not totally efcap'd this Misfortune; for how many have I known that carried competent Eftates to *North America*, neglecting Tillage, and breeding Cattle, in a few Years their Servants have been their Equals, and fometimes Superiors; fuch is the Force of Pru-

dence

dence and Industry. But as for our Country of *Carolana*, if Persons, who carry over Effects and Servants, be not fottishly foolish, or supinely negligent, they cannot fail of improving their own Fortunes, and without Injury to themselves, contribute to make others easy, and comparatively happy.

I will not say that Masters and Superintendants of any Sort or Kind, need take nothing with them, but that they will find all Things necessary and convenient to their Hands: Doubtless Common Sense will teach them, they ought to have at least Half a Years Provisions of Things necessary, until they are acquainted with the Natives, and have establish'd a Friendship and Correspondency with them : But abundance of Trouble and Expence will be sav'd in Planting this Country, which could not be well avoided in those the *English* have hitherto settled on the Continent or in their Islands. For Bread in this Country, we have a great Advantage at first coming. They may have *Indian* Corn of the Inhabitants, who have almost every where Two, and in some Places Three Crops in a Year ; and I have been very credibly inform'd, that when the New comes in, they cast away a great Part of the Old to make Room in their little Granaries. Besides all along the Coast, and 2 or 300 Miles up the Country from the Sea, they have the Root *Mandihoca*, whereof *Cassavi* Bread and Flower is made, whereupon almost all *America*

between

between the Tropicks doth subsist, (excepting what is brought them at great Expence from *Europe*, or our Northern Plantations) and which many esteem as good a Nourishment as our Manchet, and six times cheaper.

Besides, this Country naturally affords a-nother Sort of excellent Corn, which is the most like Oats of any *European* Grain, but longer and larger; and I have been assur'd by many very credible Persons, who often, out of Curiosity had divers Ways prepar'd it, that it far exceeds our best Oatmeal. This is not sown and cultivated by the *Indians*, but grows spontaneously in Marshy Places, in and by the Sides of Rivers, like Reeds or Rushes. The *Indians* when it is ripe take Handfulls, shake them into their Canows; what escapes them falling into the Water, without any further Trouble, pro-duces the next Years Crop. Rice may be there rais'd in as great Plenty as in *Ca-rolina*. For Fruits, they have not divers growing in *Europe*, which were once Stran-gers to us, and by Art and Industry in some Measure naturaliz'd; but they have others little, if at all Inferior, such as most excellent Limes or wild Lemons, and Prunes, growing in the open Fields with-out Culture, which they eat plentifully, immediately from the Trees, and keep dry for Winter Provision. Many, who have tasted both, unanimously affirm, they never did meet with either Sort in *Europe* comparable

comparable thereunto : And those dry'd will
not prove a contemptible Commodity, when
we contract Friendship with the Natives,
who being directed by us how to gather
and order them, would supply us with great
Quantities, not only for our own Subsistance
and Delight, but even for Exportation. Besides, the Tunas a most delicious Fruit, especially in hot Weather, and also not only
agreeable to the Palate, but Salubrious, and
as our *Europeans* call it, when in Maturity,
their Cordial Julep.

I now come to that Tree, I mean the
Vine, which a great Part of the World almost idolizes. I know, there have been
great Disputes amongst the learn'd, (and po-
sitively determin'd by *Mahomet* and the *Ma-
hometans* all over the World,) whither it had
not been better for Mankind it had never existed , considering how much that
noble Juice hath been abus'd, and how often it has been the Cause of numberless Ca-
lamities. For my own particular, I must
own it is my Opinion, that, next to Bread
which is the Staff of Life, it is one of the
greatest, meerly material Comforts, we in
these Northern Climates enjoy ; and having
been long thereunto accustom'd, when tranfplanted into a more Southern Country, we
shall hanker after it : And if we cannot have
good of our own Produce, we shall certainly have Recourse to Foreigners, and purchase it at any Rate, and thereby impove-
rish

rifh our Infant Colony. But thanks to Almighty GOD, who hath not only fo long, fo wonderfully, favour'd the *Englifh* Nation in their own Ifland, but takes Care even of them, who fome account their Out-cafts, tho' they have the true *Englifh* Courage, Love to their Country, and contribute, perhaps as much, to its Wealth and Welfare by their Induftry, as any equal Number, of their Rank and Quality, they have left behind. But, to put a Period to this Digreffion, Vines of divers Sorts and Kinds grow naturally in this Country. We have already difcover'd and diftinguifh'd Five or Six Sorts very different from each other; but in fuch great Plenty, that in a Thoufand Places, either upon the Continent, or in the Iflands, efpecially in or near the great Rivers, they make your Journies fhorter, by intangling your Legs, it being natural for them to run upon the Ground, unlefs they meet with Trees, up which they creep, loaded with Clufters of Grapes, of fome Sorts, commonly half a Yard, fometimes 2 Foot long. It is true fome of thefe Grapes, for want of Culture, tho' large as Damfons, have great Stones, and a tough Skin; yet they might be eafily meliorated by *European* Skill; tho' as they are, efpecially Two or Three Sorts of the fmaller Kind, are as grateful to the Palate, as moft we have in *England*; but the very worft, duly managed, produces Brandy, hardly inferior to any

in

in *Europe*; so that had we Veſſels to diſtill,
and skilful Operators, we might ſoon abate
the Price of that Liquor in *England*, and our
Plantations and keep a ſufficient Reſerve for
ourſelves.

And further, when we have once obtain'd the Skill of Meliorating the Grapes, we
ſhall alſo produce not only as good Wine,
but alſo as good Raiſons, as in moſt Countries of *Europe*; the Climate being admirably adapted thereunto; and thereby not
only ſupply ourſelves and Neighbouring Colonies, but ſomewhat abate the Expence of
our Mother, good *Old England*, from whom
we proceed, and upon whom we, and (I
hope and believe) all our other Colonies,
will not only acknowledge their ſole Dependance, but ever deſire, with the utter-
moſt of their Power, to manifeſt, upon all
Occaſions, their Love and Gratitude.

But Corn and Drink are not ſufficient for
Engliſhmen, who are us'd to feed upon
good Beef, Mutton, Bacon, Veal and Pork:
Therefore for the Encouragement of ſuch as
ſhall hereafter inhabit this Province, they
will find good Beef, and conſequently Veal,
there being a Sort of Kine natural to this
Country, which, though they differ a little
in Shape from ours (having a Bunch upon
their Shoulders, which is delicious Food)
yet otherways are not in the leaſt inferior to
our Bulls and Cows, and they make them
Oxen when they pleaſe; and by dry Fodder
ſtall

ftall Oxen like thofe in *England*; but, as
they are without Art and Care, they almoft
equal our grafs Cattle. There are alfo Sheep
of the *Spanifh* Breed in good Numbers, whofe
Flefh is as good as ours, and their Wooll
better ; as alfo Hogs very plentiful, on the
Sea-Coaft efpecially, and fome within Land,
tho' not fo numerous, Acorns, Chefnuts, and
other Mafts abounding in this Country, render them more grateful Food, (as all who
have fed upon them affirm) than ours in *England*; and fit for Exportation for the Iflands.

Next to Food we are to confider a very
material Circumftance, and that is, Cattle
for Draught, and Horfes for Riding, which
are carried into the Plantations, whither on
the Continent, or in the Iflands. Thefe are
already prepar'd unto your Hands, with no
great Trouble and Expence. For Horfes, they
are commonly us'd among the *Indians* on
the Weft-fide of the great River for Riding
and Burthens, as amongft us, tho' they
have not improv'd them for Draught, being totally ignorant of Coaches, Waines,
Carts or Plows, unto all which they may
foon by Care and Skill be adapted. And
the Price of a good Horfe will not amount
unto above Five Shillings of our *European*
Commodities at firft Coft, as I am well
affur'd by Traders, who have been offer'd
a very good one for a very ordinary Hat-
chet. And as for Oxen for Plow and Cart,
when their young Males are caftrated, they
will

will be as tame and as serviceable as our
Oxen; tho' amongst the *Tartars*, from whom
these Kine originally came, the great Bulls,
of almost twice the Strength and Bigness of
ours, are by them so far tam'd, that they
imploy them to draw their Houses or Huts
put upon Carts many Hundred Miles, as
they have occasion to remove their Habitations, which is only for convenient Pasture,
marching in the Winter to the South, in
the Summer to the North. This Sort of
Cattle are not only useful for Food and Labour, but also for their Hair, or rather
Wool, which is very long, very thick, and
very fine; and I think, as do many others
who understand the Use of it, for Hats,
Cloathing, and divers other Necessaries,
with some small suitable Addition or Mix-
tures, is preferrable to Common Wool.
Their Skins may be partly imported to
England, and partly imploy'd in our own
Colony for Harness, Boots, Shoes, and many other Uses.

Besides, we are near *New Mexico*, all which
Country generally imploy for Carriage
mighty great and strong Mules, produc'd by
Assinegos, or Male Asses, many of which
there are of abundantly greater Bigness,
Strength, and Mettle, than in *Europe*, which
with the Mares of that Country would produce an excellent Breed, if it be thought
advantageous to raise them.

There

There are several Tracts of Land in this Country that would suit very well with Cammels, many of which are imploy'd by the *Spaniards*, especially in *Peru* and *Terra Firma*, or the South-part of the Gulph of *Mexico*. They have them mostly from the *Canary* Islands, and some from *Africa*. They stand well in *America*, are very useful, and a very little Trouble and Charge will subsist them.

The wild Animals of this Country, besides the Elk or Buffalo abovemention'd, are Panthers, Bears, Wolves, Wild Catts, none of which are hurtful to Mankind; Deer of divers Sorts, Bever, Otter, Fox, Racoons, Squirrels, Martins, and Conies between ours and Hares in great Abundance; as likewise a Rat with a Bag under its Throat, wherein it conveys its Young when forc'd to fly. All these are useful for their Furrs or Skins, and some for Food ; but I think it not material nor consistent with my design'd Brevity to enter into a particular Description of them : No more than of the following Birds or Wild Fowl found all over the Country, Sea-shore, and Rivers, such as Eagles, Gosse Hawks, Falcons, Jer-Falcons and most other Birds of Prey that are in *Europe* ; Great Companies of Turkies, Bustards, Pheasants, Partridges, Pidgeons, Thrushes, Black-birds, Snipes, Cranes, Swans, Geese, Ducks, Teale, Pelicans, Parrots, and many other Sorts of curious Birds differing from ours.

For

For Cloathing, tho' we may reasonably suppose, that by our Correspondence with our Native Country, we may be supply'd therewith, as also with Beds, Carpets, Coverlets, &c. yet it would not be amiss, if in the Infancy of this Colony , the poorer Sort were encourag'd to manufacture the Wool of Sheep and Kine, as also Cotton, to supply their urgent Necessities. Hats may be made of the long soft Hair of the Kine mix'd, if need be, with a little of the Hair or Wool of *Bever* , both which are in great Plenty , and easily procur'd, and nothing wanting but a few Artists to manufacture them as in *England*.

I have receiv'd Information from divers Persons, who unanimously affirm, That some of the most civiliz'd Nations in this Country, especially of the better Sort, are cloathed with a Substance like good Course , serviceable Linnen, very White. Upon Inquiry , they found it was made with the inward Bark of Trees, which grow plentifully there, and is as becoming as most of the ordinary Linnen of *Europe* ; and by the Relation of the Natives no less durable. Of the same and other Barks, they make Thread, Cords and Ropes , of divers Lengths, and Magnitudes , which might be greatly improv'd by our *English* Planters.

Olives would certainly grow here as well as in *New Spain*, where they thrive, especially in those Parts contiguous to our Country
try

try, and are not inferior, either for eating
or making Oil, to thofe of *Spain* and *Portugal* : As alfo Almonds, feveral affirming,
particularly, I remember, the famous *Acofta*
writes concerning the Productions of the
Weft-Indies, where he long refided, that they
far exceed thofe of *Spain* or any other Part
of *Europe* : But for political Reafons, both
they and Vines are forbidden to be us'd for
the Production of Oil or Wine.

Currants alfo would probably profper in
this Country, the Climate being much of
the fame Nature and Latitude with the
Iflands of *Zant*, and *Cephelonia*, from whence
we now do generally bring them ; and the
famous City of *Corinth*, from which they
derive their Name, and from whence they
were tranfplanted to the foremention'd Iflands;
the *Latin* Name being *Vva Corinthiacæ*, or
Grapes of *Corinth*, which we corruptly call
Currants, inftead of *Corinths*. Thefe Three
Commodities were thought fo needful, that
King *Charles* II. with the Advice of His
Council, gave great Encouragement, in His
Patent for *Carolina*, to the Proprietors, Planters or any others, who fhould produce and
import them to *England* ; As alfo Capers and
fome other Commodities there mention'd.

Cotton grows wild in the Codd and in
great Plenty, may be manag'd and improv'd
as in our Iflands, and turn to as great
Account ; and in Time perhaps manufactu-

G   red

red either in the Country or in *Great-Britain*, which will render it a Commodity ftill more valuable.

Pearls are to be found in great Abundance in this Country : The *Indians* put fome Value upon them, but not fo much as on the colour'd Beads we bring them. On the whole Coaft of this Province , for 200 Leagues, there are many vaft Beds of Oyfters, which breed Pearls, as has been found in divers Places : But, which is very remarkable , far from the Sea in frefh Water Rivers and Lakes, there is a Sort of Shell-Fifh between a Mufcle and a Pearl Oyfter, wherein are found abundance of Pearls, and many of an unufual Magnitude. The *Indians*, when they take the Oyfters , broil them over the Fire 'till they are fit to eat, keeping the large Pearls they find in them, which by the Heat are tarnifh'd and lofe their Native Luftre : But when we have taught them the right Method, doubtlefs it would be a very profitable Trade. There are two Places we already know within Land, in each of which there is a great Pearl Fifhery. One about 120 Leagues up the River *Mefchacebe*, on the Weft-fide, in a Lake made by the River of the *Naches*, about 40 Miles from its Mouth, where they are found in great Plenty and many very large. The other on the River *Chiaha*, which runs into the *Coza* or *Cuffaw* River

(as

(as our *English* calls it) and which comes
from the N. E. and after a Course of some
Hundred Miles disimbogues into the Gulph
of *Florida*, about 100 Miles to the East of
the *Meschacebe*.

The judicious and faithful Writer of the
famous Expedition of *Ferdinando Soto*, who
was therein from the Beginning unto the
End, acquaints us, That when they came
to *Cutifachia*, the chief of that Country finding they valu'd Pearl, offer'd to load all their
Horses therewith, which were at least Two
Hundred. And to confirm them in the Be-
lief of what they advanc'd, carried them
unto Two of their chief Temples, where
they found vast Quantities, but took only
Fourteen Bushels for a Shew to the *Havana*,
and other of the *Spanish* Dominions, to encourage the Peopling of this Colony, not
being willing to incumber their Horses with
more, their Welfare and Success depending
much upon their Horsemen, the *Indians* being abundantly more afraid of them than
the Foot; whose Guns being useless after a
short Time for want of Powder, they only
made Use of Cross-Bows. And *Garzilassa*,
who was not with *Soto*, but writ only upon Memoirs he receiv'd from divers who
were present, gives a more full Account of
the prodigious Quantity of Pearls in that
Country, affirming, the *Spaniards* calculated
them to amount unto a Thousand Bushels.

And

And afterwards when the *Spaniards* at *Chia-ha* were gathering Oysters for their Food, they found many large Pearls, and and one particularly that was priz'd at Four Hundred Ducats, not having loft the leaft of its Luftre, being taken out of a Raw Oyfter. And that one *Terron* a *Spaniard* had above Six Pounds Weight of Pearl very large, and moftly of a beautiful Luftre, and were valu'd at Six Thoufand Ducats.

It need not feem incredible, that Pearl fhould be taken in frefh Water Lakes and Rivers, there being many Relations of unqueftionable Reputation, which declare, very good and large Pearls are found in divers Parts of *China*, and the Countries to the Weft and South-Weft of their great Wall (with which Quotations I will not enlarge this Difcourfe) as will appear by reading the *China Atlas* of *Martinius*, *Marcus Paulus Venetus*, and other credible Writers on Lakes and frefh Water Rivers.

Cochineal is a Commodity of great Value, very neceffary as the World goes, and cofts this Nation annually great Sums of Money, which may be all fav'd, there being in this Province fufficient to furnifh both us, and our Neighbours, who are no lefs fond of it than ourfelves. There have been great Enquiries, and many Difputes, about the Original of this Commodity, which is the famous Ingredient for dying in Grain, the

Purple

Purple and Scarlet Colours, generally efteemed by opulent and civiliz'd Nations.

This noble Ingredient for dying, is produc'd by a Tree or Shrub call'd the Tunal or Tuna, of which there are divers Sorts ; fome bearing an excellent Fruit very pleafant and wholfome. It is made of certain Infects breeding in the Fruit of this Plant, when it is well husbanded, and are thereunto faftn'd, cover'd with a fmall fine Webb, which doth Compafs them about, and when come to Maturity they eat through it, fall off the Tree, and being carefully gather'd, dry'd, and curioufly put up, are fent to *Spain*, and thence diftributed to moft civiliz'd Parts of *Europe*, and *Afia*. *Acofta* tells us, That in the Fleet wherein he return'd from *Mexico*, that Province only, fhipp'd 5677 Arobes, each whereof is 25 *l.* Weight, and valu'd at 283750 Peices of Eight. The Cochineal is of two Sorts, one growing Wild, which they call Silvefter. This, tho' it gives a good Price, is far fhort of that, which is duly cultivated in Gardens and Fields, much after the manner the *Englifh* do Tobacco in their Plantations. This Province both on the Eaft and Weft-fide of the *Mefchacebe* , from the Gulph of *Mexico*, fome Hundred Miles up the Country, abounds with all Sorts of Tunals, or Tuna's (as fome ftyle them) ufually found in the Province of *Mexico*, which borders upon it , and is only divided by an imaginary Line, from the Degrees of 30 to

36.

36. When this Country is settled, and we
set upon this Manufacture, the *Indians* may
be very helpful unto us, it being easy Labour , and wherein we need only imploy
their Women and Young People, if their
Men, who are generally very lazy, decline
it.

The Plant of which Indico is made , is
very frequent in most of the Southern Parts
of this Country, and may possibly produce
better than that made in our Islands of *Jamaica*, &c. This Province being in the same
Latitude with *Agra* and *Byana*, Territories
in the great *Mogul*'s Country, whose Indico is
accounted the best of its Kind in the World,
and is double the Price of ours. It is easily made , and the *Indians* may be assisting
to us herein, if we think fit to undertake
it. Besides if we believe that judicious natural Historian *Hernando*, there is in *Mexico*,
and consequently here (being much the same
Climate) a Plant or little Shrub, which produces an Indico abundantly more noble, and
the Colour more lively, than that which is
the Common Indico. This the *Spaniards* call
Azul, as being like Ultramarine.

Ambergris or grey Amber, is often found
upon this Coast from the Cape of *Florida* to
Mexico, which is of great Value. The best
(for there are divers Sorts) is of equal
worth to its weight in Gold. This is agreed
upon by the Learned, to be a Bitumen or
Naptha, which comes from certain Springs
or

or Fountains, that empty themselves into the Sea, and is coagulated by the Salt-Water, as Succinum, commonly call'd Amber, from another Sort of Bitumen or Naptha, and in Storms cast upon the Coast. The same Ambergris is also found upon the East-side of the Cape or *Peninsula* of *Florida*, the *Bahama* Islands, in the *East-Indies*, and *Brasil*, and sometimes great Lumps, even upon the Coast of *Cornwall* and *Ireland* And among others, I have read of a Piece weighing Eighty Pounds, cast upon the Coast of *Cornwall*, in the Reign of King *Charles* I. which was bigger, till diminish'd by the Countryman who found it, by greasing his Cart Wheels, and Boots, but discover'd accidentally by an intelligent Gentleman, who riding by one of his Carts, and perceiving a very grateful Smell, enquir'd of the Man whence it proceeded; he told him he had found a nasty Greese on the Shore, which he hop'd would have sav'd him the Expence of Kitchin Stuff and Tarr for Carts, Harness, and Boots, but it was of so poysonous a Smell, that they were not able to endure it. The Gentleman desiring to see the Remainder, found it what he expected, purchas'd it at a very easy Rate, presented it unto the Queen, and was requited in Places or Employments far• beyond the Value of it.

There is found in great Quantities upon the same Coast on the Shore to the East and

West

Weſt of the *Meſchacebe*, eſpecially after high
South Winds, a Sort of Stone Pitch by the
Spaniards call'd Copec, which they likewiſe
find in the *South-Sea* upon the Coaſt of *Peru*.
They mix it with Greeſe to make it more
liquid, and uſe it as Pitch for their Veſſels,
and affirm it to be better in hot Countries,
not being apt to melt with the Heat of the
Sun or Weather. And at *Trinadad* a large
Iſland over against the great River of *Oronogue*, there is a Mountain of the ſaid Subſtance, of which Sir *Walter Raleigh* gives
an Account in his Expedition, ſo fatal unto
him, of the Diſcovery of the ſaid River;
and ſeveral Navigators ſince have done the
ſame. *Acoſta*, the famous Author of the natural Hiſtory of the *West-Indies*, affirms it to
be generated of an Oil, which empties itſelf,
he knows not how, into ſeveral Parts of the
Ocean, in ſo great Quantities, that the Sailors, when at a Loſs, know where they are
by its Floating on the Sea, or the Smell thereof, which, he ſays, they ſcented at a conſiderable
Diſtance. The *Engliſh* ſent to diſcover the
River *Meſchacebe*, affirm the ſame, and that
they found it in two Places, which I have well
mark'd. Moreover, that the Sea was cover'd
with an Oil or Slime, as they ſtile it, which
had a very ſtrong Smell for many Leagues
together. I ſuppoſe they had much the
ſame Conceptions with the Countryman be-
forementiond'd, and therefore their Curioſity
did not prompt them to take it up, and
examine

examine its Qualities ; tho' probably, it might be of the fame Nature and Ufe, with that of divers Wells in the Province of *Adierbigian* in *Perfia*, near the *Cafpian* Sea, whence they fetch it many Hundred Miles on Camels, being us'd to burn it in Lamps inftead of Oil, it emitting a moft grateful and wholfome Odour. I might add Sperma Cete Whales, out of which that Subftance is extracted, are fometimes kill'd by the Natives, and fometimes by Storms, as it were fhipwreck'd on the Shore, but either of thefe feldom happening, there can be no great Dependance or Expectation from them.

Salt is of great Ufe, efpecially unto *Europeans*, without which they cannot well fubfift, being accuftom'd thereunto from their Infancy, and without which Food hath no Relifh. Befides it is fuppos'd, that it prevents Putrefaction, and innumerable Difeafes ; and in Foreign Countries, where it hath been wanting, they have greatly fuffer'd. It is moreover neceffary to preferve Fifh and Flefh, which without it cannot be long kept fweet. In this Country it may be eafily and abundantly procur'd. We know divers Places, on both Sides of the River, where there are many Springs and Lakes, producing plentifully excellent Salt; and alfo one Mine of Rock-Salt, almoft clear as Criftal, and probably there may be many more of the fame. By thefe we may not only fupply ourfelves with what

is

is neceſſary for our ordinary daily Food, du-ring the Winter or other Seaſons, but alſo furniſh our (I may call them Neighbour) Plantations in the Iſlands , (we not being very remote from them,) with Fiſh, Fleſh, and Salt; when by Reaſon of War, or o-ther ſiniſter Accidents, they cannot receive due and expected Recruits from *England* or elſewhere.

Silk is a Commodity of great Uſe in *Eng-land* for many Manufactures, it being im-ported to us from *France*, *Italy*, *Sicily*, *Turky*, and the *Eaſt-Indies*; and there is no Fo-reign Commodity, which exhauſts more of our Treaſure. I am not ſo vain as to pro-miſe, this Country can furniſh *Great-Bri-tain* with ſo much Silk, as is therein manu-factured, which would amount to above half a Million or a Million *Sterling* annually : But if this Province is ever ſettled, (it abounding in moſt Parts with Foreſts of Mulberry Trees, both White and Red) and we keep a good Correſpondence with the Natives, which is both our Duty and Intereſt, certainly a con-ſiderable Quantity of Silk may be here pro-duced. It hath been already experimented, in *South Carolina*, by Sir *Nathaniel Johnſon* and others, which would have return'd to great Account, but that they wanted Hands, Labourers being not to be hir'd but at a vaſt Charge. Yet if the Natives or *Negroes* were employ'd, who delight in ſuch eaſy light Labours, we could have that done;
for

for lefs than One Shilling, which cofts them
more then fix. Now I appeal to all good
Englishmen, if we can raife only a Tenth Part
of the Silk expended in *Great-Britain*, &c. and
perhaps half an Age hence the Fifth, whether it would not be very beneficial to our
Native Country, and a little Check upon
others, with whom we deal in that Commodity, by letting them know, if they are
unreafonable and exorbitant in their Demands, that we may in a fhort Time fupply ourfelves, in a great Meafure, from
our own Plantations? I am not ignorant
there are feveral Sorts of Silks, proper for
divers diftinct Ufes, as of *China*, *Bengale*,
and other Parts of the *East-Indies*, *Perfia*,
Turkey, *Naples*, and *Sicily*; for what Manufactures ours is moft proper, I know not;
but it hath given a good Price, and Experience may teach us to raife for more Ufes
than one. I would advife my Countrymen,
when they fet up this Manufacture, to imi-
tate the *Chinefe*, who fow the Mulberry
Seeds as we do Pot-herbs, and to mow
thofe of one Years growth for the Young
Silk Worms, the Leaves being fhort and
tender, fit Food for them when frefh hatch-
ed; and the Second for them when in their
Infancy, as I may defervedly ftile it; when
grown ftrong they may be fupply'd with
Leaves from the Trees; which Method fe-
cures them from the Difeafes, whereunto
they are obnoxious, when fed from the
Beginning,

Beginning, with great rank Leaves, faves much Trouble, and leffens the Number of Hands to attend them, which is the greateft Expence.

Hemp and Flax are not only Materials for divers Manufactures in *England*, but exceedingly ufeful, and indeed almoft neceffary in a new Colony, to fupply them with Courfe Linnens of divers Kinds, whereof, if we made much and finer, it would be no Injury to our Mother *England*, who hath moft from Foreign Parts; as alfo Cordage, Thread, Twine for Nets, and other Ufes. The Plants which produce Hemp and Flax, are very common in this Country, and abundantly fufficient to fupply not only the Neceffities thereof, but likewife of the whole *Britifh* Nation. Befides we have a Grafs, as they call it Silk Grafs, which makes very pretty Stuffs, fuch as come from the *Eaft-Indies*, which they call *Herba* Stuffs, whereof a Garment was made for Queen *Elizabeth*, whofe Ingredient came from Sir *Walter Raleigh*'s Colony, by him call'd *Virginia*, Now *North-Carolina*, a Part of this Province, which, to encourage Colonies and Plantations, fhe was pleas'd to wear for divers Weeks.

This Country affords excellent Timber for Building Ships, as Oak, Fir, Cedar, Spruce, and divers other Sorts: And as I faid before, Flax and Hemp for Cordage and Sails; as likewife Iron for Nails and Anchors. But
with-

without Tarr, Pitch, and Rosin, a Ship can never be well equipp'd; wherefore there are divers Places in this Country near the Sea and great Rivers, which were otherwise useless, being the most sandy barren Parts of the Country, wherein that Tree grows which produces all those Materials for Naval Architecture; the same Tree likewise produces Turpentine, which is no contemptible Commodity. This Tree being peirc'd, and a Vessel conveniently fastn'd unto or plac'd under the Aperture, the Turpentine distills plentifully into it: If cut, and a Hole made under the Tree in the Sand (for in that Soil it generally grows) the Turpentine by the Influence of the Air and Sun, without any further Trouble, becomes good Rosin. Pitch and Tarr are made by cutting the dry Trees into Scantlings, taking the Knotts of old Trees fallen, and the rest of the Wood rotted, burning, as you make here Charcoal, covering with Turf, and leaving Orifices for as much Air as will keep the Fire from extinguishing. The Moisture partly Aqueous, partly Bituminous, runs by a gentle Descent into a Pit, what swims is Tarr, which inflam'd to a certain Degree and extinguish'd is Pitch.

I suppose it will not seem a Grievance for us to build Ships in this Country to bring Home our Native Commodities, when it is allow'd in our other Plantations, and sup-

supposed to save us a vast Expence of
Boards, Masts, Yards, &c. which were formerly brought us from *Norway* and *Sweden*,
where its well known, that three Parts in
four are pay'd for in ready Money, and
not a Fourth in our own Native Commodities or Manufactures. Besides the Pitch,
Tarr, Rosin and Turpentine, the Produce
of the Trees beforemention'd, the Ashes
which remain, with; a very small Accession, and little Trouble, will make Pot-Ashes,
no contemptible Commodity, and which
costs *England* every Year to Foreign Parts,
(as I have been inform'd by competent
Judges) above Fifty Thousand Pounds: But
I will not insist further hereon, or mani-
fest what great Quantities hereof may easily be made, and how much stronger, than
most of that we import from *Russia, Livo-
nia, Courland, Prussia, Sweden, Norway,* and
other Countries; we having so many other
valuable Commodities to imploy our Time
and Labour about.

The mention of Pot-Ashes, so much us'd
by Soap-Boilers and Dyers, brings to mind
several Materials for Dying. This Country
affords Logwood, otherwise call'd Campeche-
Wood, and many other Dying Woods,
Fustick, &c. which, divers, who try'd them,
affirm, are not inferior to those growing on
the opposite side of the Gulph, in the *Spanish* Dominions, whence we have hitherto
receiv'd them, with much Charge, Hazard
and

and Trouble. There are besides the Woods
in this Country, divers Shrubs and Plants,
whose Roots even as us'd by the *Indians*,
die the finest and most durable Colours,
Black, Yellow, Blue, and especially Red;
which if planted, and cultivated, as Ma-
ther Wood, and Saffron amongst us, might
probably be beneficial unto the Underta-
kers.

Some Persons are very inquisitive, whether this Country produces Gemms : I pre-
tend not to the Knowledge of Diamonds,
Rubies and Balasses, Saphires, Emeralds, or
Chrysolites; all that have come to my
Knowledge are Amethists, of which there
are very fine and large, and to the *West-
Turchoises*, thought to be as large and good
as any in the known World; and possibly
upon Inquiry and diligent Search, others
may be found.

We have an Account of *Lapis Lazuli*,
which is an Indication, as Mine-Masters
generally affirm, that Gold is not far off.
I never did see or hear of any *Lapis Lazuli*
extraordinary good, but had visible Streaks,
or Veins of pure Gold: But tho' it is not
ordinarily reckon'd amongst precious Stones,
yet, if good in its Kind, it is sold for its
Weight in Gold, to make that glorious
Azure call'd Ultramarine, without which no
marvelous, and durable Painting can be
made. And Monsieur *Turnefort* in his Voyage to the *Levant* observes, That besides
that

that *Lazuli* is found in Gold-Mines, there
seem to be in this Stone some Threads of
Gold as it were still uncorrupted.

I had almost forgot to communicate two
Commodities one for the Health, the other
for the Defence of our Bodies. The former
is a Shrub call'd Caffine, much us'd and
celebrated by the Natives, the Leaves whereof dry'd will keep very long, of which several People have had many Years Experience. The *Indians* drink plentifully thereof,
(as we do Tea in *Europe*, and the *Chineses*,
from whom it is exported) more especially
when they undertake long and dangerous
Expeditions against their Enemies, affirming,
it takes away Hunger, Thirst, Weariness,
and that tormenting Passion, Fear, for
Twenty-four Hours : And none amongst
them are allow'd to drink it, but those,
who have well deserv'd by their Military
Atcheivments, or otherwise obtain'd the Favour of their petty Royteletts.

The latter is Salt-Peter, which may probably be here procur'd, cheap and plentifully,
there being at certain Seasons of the Year
most prodigious Flights of Pidgeons, I have
been assur'd by some who have seen them,
above a League long, and half as broad.
These come, many Flocks successively,
much the same Course, roost upon the Trees
in such Numbers, that they often break
the Boughs, and leave prodigious Heaps of
Dung behind them ; from which, with
good

good Management, and very little Expence, great Quantities of the beſt Salt-Peter may be extracted.

Having given an Account of the moſt valuable Animals and Vegetables this Country produces, for Food and other Uſes, as well as Materials for Trade and Manufacture, Some, who have heard or read of the immenſe Riches in Gold and Silver, that are annually exported from *Peru*, *Mexico*, and other Territories of the *Spaniards* in *America* to *Spain*, and of the incredible Quantities of Gold that have been imported from *Brazil* into *Portugal*, for above Thirty Years paſt (The Benefit of which all the World knows we have ſhar'd in) will be ready to enquire, whither the like Mines exiſt in this Country? Whereunto it may be anſwer'd; were there no ſuch Mines, yet where there is ſo good, rich, fertil, Land; ſo pure and healthful an Air and Climate; ſuch an Abundance of all Things for Food and Raiment; valuable Materials for Domeſtick and Foreign Trade; theſe Advantages alone, if induſtriouſly improv'd, and prudently manag'd, will in the Event, bring in Gold and Silver by the Ballance of Trade, as in the Caſe of *England* and *Holland*; who without Mines of Gold or Silver, are perhaps the richeſt Nations, for the Quantity of Land they poſſeſs, and Number of Inhabitants, in the whole Commercial World. And its well

H   known

known, that we and some other industrious *Europeans* receive, in Exchange for our
Commodities, the greatest Part of the Wealth,
which comes in Bullion from the *West-Indies*, either to *Spain* or *Portugal*. But not to
discourage any whose Genius inclines them
to the Discovery and Working of Mines, I
will add, Who knows, but we may have
here as rich as any in the known World?
Who hath searched? As *Tacitus* said of *Ger-
many* in the Heighth of the *Roman* Empire;
I mean the Reign of the great *Trajan*, Sixteen Hundred Years since. Yet afterwards
there were found, Gold, Silver, Lead, Tin,
Copper, Quick-silver, Spelter, Antimo-
ny, Vitriol, the best in the World, Blue,
Green, and White; besides many other Mineral Productions, which are now wrought
to the great Advantage of divers Sovereign
Princes and their Subjects.

But to make a more particular Reply to
such Suggestions. They may be assur'd, that
Copper is in Abundance, and so fine, that
it is found in Plates, Bitts and Pieces very
pure without Melting, of which considerable
Quantities have been gather'd on the Surface of the Earth. And they who have
tried some of the Oar affirm, by common
Methods, it gives above Forty *per Cent.*
The famous *Alonso Barba*, who hath given
an admirable Account of the Mines the
Spaniards have discover'd in *America*, and
the Ways of working them, assures us, that
besides

beſides the Mines abounding in that Metal
near the Surface of the Earth, they found,
digging deeper, that they prov'd the richeſt Silver Mines, they have hitherto diſcover'd. And all agree, the Gold extracted out of Copper, is Finer, of a higher
Tincture, or more Caratts, than that ex-
tracted from Silver or any other Metal;
and that without the tedious Proceſs of burning ſeveral Times before Melting, imploy'd
conſtantly, in order to the extracting Copper,
by *Swedes* and other *European* Nations.

Lead is there in great Quantities. What
has already been diſcover'd, is more than
ſufficient for Common Uſe, and the Oar affords Sixty *per Cent*.

I need not perhaps mention Coal, the
Country ſo much abounding in Wood.
But becauſe in ſome Caſes, that may be
more uſeful and proper than Wood, I will
add, That in many Places there are known
to be Mines of Pit-Coal, like that we have
from *Scotland*, *Wales*, and ſome of our Inland Countries in *England*.

Iron Oar is in abundance of Places near
the Surface of the Earth; and ſome Parts
produce Iron, little inferior to Steel in Good-
neſs, and uſeful in many Caſes, wherein Steel
is commonly imploy'd, as divers atteſt, who
have made Trials thereof.

This Country affords another profitable
Commodity or Mineral, which is Quick-ſil-;
ver. We have Knowledge of two Mines

H 2   one

one on the Weft ; the other on the Eaft of the great River ; and doubtlefs many more might be found if enquir'd after. The Natives make no other Ufe thereof, than to paint their Faces and Bodies therewith , in Time of War, and great Feftivals. This we call Quick-filver, is the Mother of Quick-filver, or the Mineral out of which it is ex-tracted, and is a Rock of a Scarlet or Pur-ple Colour ; which being broke and diftill'd in Earthen Pots , the Necks whereof are put into others almoft full of Water , the latter, for the greater Part of each of them in the Ground, then are plac'd in Rows, al-moft contiguous, cover'd with fpray Wood, which burning drives the Quickfilver by Def-cent out of the Mineral into the Water. Three or Four Men will tend fome Thou-fands of thefe Pots. The great Trouble is in digging ; all the Expence not amount-ing unto a Tenth Part of the Value of the Produce.

And it is generally obferv'd by all, who write well on Mines, Metals, and Minerals, That tho' Silver be often found, where there is no Cinnabar of Quick-filver in its Neigh-bourhood, yet Cinnabar is rarely found but Silver Mines are near. This Cinnabar or Ver-million, tho' a good Commodity in itfelf in *Europe*, and among the Savages, for fome pick'd chofen Pieces, is chiefly valuable for the Quick-filver it produces; efpecially if we ever obtain a free Trade with the *Spaniards*;
and

and will be beyond all Exception for our
and their mutual Benefit: For moſt of the
Silver Oar in *America*, mix'd with Quick-ſil-
ver, produces almoſt double the Quantity of
Metal, it would do only by Melting; ſo
that the *Spaniards* have annually ſix or eight
Thouſand Quintals, or Hundred Weight,
brought unto them from the Bottom of the
Adriatick Gulph, out of the Territories of
the Emperor, and the *Venetians*, *viz.* from
Iſtria, *Styria*, *Carinthia*, *Carniola*, *Friuli*, and
Dalmatia. We can ſell it them, and deliver
it for half what that coſts, which comes from
Europe, they being within ſix or eight Days
ſail of the Place where it is produc'd. And
for *Mexico* we can deliver it for the Mines
in *New Biſcay*, &c. in the River of *Palmes*,
or *Rio Bravo*, otherwiſe call'd the River of
Eſcondido: As alſo by the River of the *Houmas*, which enters the *Meſchacebe*, 100 Leag.
from its Mouth, on the Weſt-ſide, after a
Courſe of above 500 Miles. It is a very
large deep River, Navigable at leaſt 300
Miles by Ships; afterwards unto its Heads
by Barks and flat-bottom'd Boats, having
no Falls. It proceeds from that Narrow
Ridge of low Mountains, which divides this
Country, and the Province of *New Mexico.*
The Hills may be paſs'd not only by Men
and Horſes, but alſo by Waggons in leſs
than half a Day. On the other ſide are
ſmall Navigable Rivers, which, after a ſhort
Courſe of 30 or 40 Miles, empty themſelves
into

into the abovesaid *Rio Bravo*, which comes from the most Northerly Part of *New Mexico*, in 38 Degrees of Latitude, and enters the Sea at the N. W. End of the Gulph of *Mexico*, in 27 Degrees of Latitude.

There is also another easy Passage, to the Northern Part of *New Mexico*, by the Yellow River, which about 60 Miles above its Mouth, is divided into Two great Branches; or rather those Two Branches form that great River, which is no less than the *Meschacebe*, where they are united. The North Branch proceeds from the North-West, and is call'd the River of the *Massorites*, from a great Nation who live thereon. The other which comes from the West and by South, is nam'd the River of the *Ozages*, a populous Nation of that Name inhabiting on its Banks; and their Heads proceed from the aforesaid Hills, which Part the Province of *New Mexico* from *Carolana*, and are easily passable; as are those foremention'd of the River of the *Houmas*, which may be plainly discern'd by the Map, or Chart hereunto annex'd.

But all this is insignificant to our *Plutonists*, whom nothing will satisfy besides Gold and Silver; I will therefore here declare all I know, or have receiv'd from credible Persons, and will not add a Tittle. I am well inform'd of a Place, from whence the *Indians* have brought a Mettal, (not well indeed refin'd) and that divers Times, which purified,

purified, produc'd Two Parts Silver. And I
have an Account from another, who was
with the *Indians*, and had from them inform Maſſes of ſuch like Silver, and very
fine Pale Copper, though above 200 Miles
from the Country, where the forementioned was found. I have by me Letters
from *New Jerſey*, written many Years ſince,
by a Perſon very well ſkill'd in the Refin-
ing of Metals, ſignifying, that divers Years
ſucceſſively, a Fellow, who was there of little Eſteem, took a Fancy to ramble with
the *Indians* beyond the Hills, which ſeparate
that Colony and *New York* from this Country; he always brought Home with him a
Bag, as heavy as he could well carry, of Duſt,
or rather ſmall Particles of divers Sorts of Metals very ponderous. When melted it appeared a Mixture of Metals, unto which they could
aſſign no certain Denomination; but perceiv'd
by many Trials, that it contain'd Lead, Copper, and, when refin'd, above a Third Part
Silver and Gold; for tho' the Gold was the
leaſt in Quantity, yet it was conſiderable in
Value; which is eaſily diſcover'd by any
tolerable Artiſt of a Refiner, who knows,
how to ſeparate Gold and Silver, and what
Proportion the Maſs contains of each.
There were great Pains taken, to bring
this Fellow to diſcover, where he had this,
I may call, Treaſure, it ſerving him to
drink and ſot, till he went on another Ex-

pedition;

pedition; But neither Promifes nor Importunities would prevail. Some made him Drunk, yet he ftill kept his Secret. All they could ever fifh out of him was, that about 300 Leagues South-Weft of *Jerfey*, at a certain Seafon of the Year, there fell great Torrents of Water from fome Mountains, I fuppofe from Rains, which being pafs'd over, the *Indians* wafh'd the Sand or Earth fome Diftance below the Falls, and in the Bottom remain'd this Medley of Metals: Which brings to mind what happen'd lately in *Brafil.* Several *Portuguefe* being guilty of heinous Crimes, or afraid of the Refentment of powerful Enemies, retreated from their Habitations, to the Mountains of St. *Paul*, as they call'd them, lying in between 20 and 30 Degrees of South-Latitude, above 200 Miles from their neareft Plantations, and yearly increafing, at length form'd a Government amongft themfelves. Some inquifitive Perfon perceiving, in divers Places, fomewhat glyfter, after the Canals of the Torrents, produc'd by great Rains, at a certain Time of the Year, were dry, upon Trial found it (the Sand and Filth being wafh'd away) very fine Gold. They having upon Confultation amafs'd a good Quantity thereof, made their Peace with the King of *Portugal*, and are a peculiar Jurifdiction, paying the King his Quint or Fifth, which is refery'd in all Grants
of

of the Crown of *Spain* and *Portugal* :
and are conſtantly ſupply'd by the Merchants for ready Money, with whatſoever
Commodities they want. And I am informed by divers credible Perſons, who have long
liv'd in *Portugal*, that from this otherwiſe
contemptible uſeleſs Country, is brought by
every *Brazil* Fleet above Twelve Hundred
and Fifty Thouſand Pounds *Sterl.* only in Gold.
Who knows but what happen'd to them,
may one Time or other, in like manner,
happen to the Future Inhabitants of this
Country, not yet cultivated, fully diſcover'd,
or ranſack'd by *Europeans* ?

There are in divers Parts of this Province,
Orpiment, and Sandaracha in great Quanti-
ty; and all the Writers on Metals and
Minerals affirm, they not only contain
Gold, but where they are found they are
generally the Covering of Mines of Gold or
Silver.

But ſuppoſe all that preceded is Conje-
cture, Impoſture, or Viſionary; what I
now ſuggeſt deſerves great Attention; and
when the Country is ſettled, may invite
the beſt Heads, and longeſt Purſes, to
combine, at leaſt, to make a fair Trial of
what the *Spaniards* attempted upon naked
Conjectures.

The Mines of *New Biſcay*, *Gallicia* and
New Mexico, out of which ſuch vaſt Quantities of Silver is Yearly ſent to *Spain*, beſides

fides what is detain'd for their Domeftick
Utenfils, wherein they are very magnificent,
lie contiguous to this Country. To fay nothing of Gold, whereof they have confiderable Quantities, tho' not proportionable in
Bulk or Value to the Silver. But there is
a Ridge of Hills which run almoft due
North and South between their Country
and ours, not 30 Miles broad, and in divers Places, for many Miles, abounding with
Silver Mines, more than they can work, for
want of Native *Spaniards*, and *Negroes*. And,
which is very remarkable, they unanimoufly
affirm, the further North, the Richer the
Mines of Silver are. Which brings to mind
what *Polibius*, *Livy*, *Pliny*, and many others
of the *Greek* and *Roman* Hiftorians, and
Writers of Natural Hiftory unanimoufly report; That the rich Mines in *Spain*, upon
which the *Carthaginians* fo much depended,
and which greatly inrich'd them, were in the
Afturias and *Pyrenean* Mountains, the moft
Northerly Part of *Spain*, and in a much
greater Northern Latitude, than the furtheft
Mines of *New Mexico*, near their Capital
City *St. a Fee*, fituate in about 36 Degrees.
Not but that there are more and richer
Mines more Northerly than *St. a Fee*, but
they are hinder'd from working them, by
Three or Four populous and well polic'd Na-
tions, who have beat the *Spaniards* in many
Rencounters, not to fay Battles; and for

a

a Hundred Years, they have not been able,
by their own Confeſſion, to gain from them
one Inch of Ground.

Pliny in particular affirms, That every
Year Twenty Thouſand Pounds of Gold
were brought from their Mines in *Spain* :
And that one Mine call'd *Bebello*, from the
firſt Diſcoverer, yeilded to *Hannibal*, every Day
Three Hundred Pounds Weight of Silver ;
beſides a very rich copious Mine of Mini-
um, Cinnabaris, or Vermillion, the Mother
of Quickſilver, out of which only it is ex-
tracted. He adds, That the *Romans* continued to work theſe Mines unto his Time,
which was above Three Hundred Years ;
but they were not then ſo profitable, by
Reaſon of Subterraneal Waters, which gave
them much Trouble, they having then dig-
ged Fifteen Hundred Paces into the Mountain. But what is very remarkable, and to
our preſent Purpoſe, Theſe Mines were not
in the moſt Southerly or Middle Parts of
Spain , but as above to the Northward.
Now I deſire any Intelligent Perſon, skilful
in Mineral Affairs, to aſſign a probable Reaſon, why we, who are on that Side of the
Ridge of Hills obverted to the Riſing Sun,
which was always (how juſtly I know
not) reckon'd to abound in Mettals and Minerals, more than thoſe expos'd to the Setting Sun, may not hope for, and expect as
many and as rich Mines, as any the *Spanin-*
ards

ards are Masters of, on the other or West-side of these Mountains? Especially since several of the *Spanish* Historians and Naturalists observe, that the Mines on the Eastern side of the Mountain of *Potosi* in *Peru*, are much more numerous and rich, than those on the Western.

APPENDIX.

APPENDIX.

AN
EXTRACT
OF THE
CHARTER
Granted by
King *CHARLES* I.

To Sir ROBERT HEATH.

CHARLES *by the Grace of* GOD, &c.
*To all to whom thefe Prefents fhall
come Greeting.*

HEREAS, Our Trufty and Well-
beloved Subject and Servant, Sir
Robert Heath, Knight, Our Attorney General, being excited
with a laudable Zeal for the pro-
pagating the Chriftian Faith, the Enlarge-
ment

ment of Our Empire and Dominions, and the Increafe of Trade and Commerce of Our Kingdom, has humbly befought Leave of Us, by his own Induftry and Charge, to tranfport an ample Colony of Our Subjects, &c. unto a certain Country hereafter defcrib'd, in the Parts of *America*, between the Degrees of 31 and 36, of *Northern* Latitude inclufively, not yet cultivated or planted, &c.

KNOW ye therefore, That We favouring the pious and laudable Purpofe of Our faid Attorney, of our fpecial Grace, certain Knowledge, and mere Motion, have given, granted and confirm'd, and by this Our prefent *Charter* do give, grant and confirm unto the faid Sir *Robert Heath* Knight, his Heirs, and Affignes, for ever, All that River or Rivulet of St. *Mattheo* on the *South* Part, and all that River or Rivulet of *Paffo Magno* on the *North* Part, and all Lands, Tenements, and Hereditaments, lying, being, and extending between or within the faid two Rivers, by the Tract there unto the Ocean on the *Eaftern* and *Weftern* Parts, fo far forth and as much as the Continent there extends itfelf, with every of their Appurtenances. And alfo all thofe Iflands of *Veanis* and *Bahama.* And all other Iflands and Iflets near thereto, and lying *Southward* of and from the faid Continent, all which lie within 31 and 36 Degrees of *Northern* Latitude inclufively. And all and fingular Havens of Ships, Roads and Creeks of the Sea, to the faid Rivers, Iflands

Iſlands and Lands belonging, and all
Grounds, Lands, Woods, Lakes and Rivers
within the Regions, Iſlands and Limits a-
foreſaid, ſituate or being; with all Kinds of
Fiſhes whatſoever, Whales, Sturgeons, and
other Royal Fiſh and Fiſhings in the Sea
and Rivers. And all Veins, Mines, Pits, as
well open as ſhut, of Gold, Silver, Gems,
precious Stones, and other Stones, Metals or
Things whatſoever, within the ſaid Region,
Territory, Iſlands or Limits aforeſaid, found
or to be found. And all Patronages and Ad-
vowſons of all Churches, which, by Increaſe
of Chriſtian Religion, ſhall hereafter happen
to be built within the ſaid Region, Territory,
Iſland and Limits aforeſaid; with all and
ſingular, and with as ample Rights, Juriſ-
dictions, Privileges, Prerogatives, Royalties,
Liberties, Immunities, Royal Rights and
Franchiſes whatſoever, as well by Sea as
Land, within the ſaid Region, Territory,
Iſlands and Limits aforeſaid. To have, uſe,
exerciſe and enjoy, in as ample Manner, as
any Biſhop of *Durham* in Our Kingdom of
England, ever heretofore have, held, uſed or
enjoyed, or of Right ought or could have,
uſe or enjoy.

AND him, the ſaid Sir *Robert Heath*, his Heirs
and Aſſigns, We do by theſe Preſents, for
Us, Our Heirs and Succeſſors, make, create
and conſtitute the true and abſolute Lords
and Proprietors of the ſaid Region and Territory aforeſaid, and of all other the Premiſes,

mifes, faving always the Faith and Allegi-
ance due to Us, Our Heirs and Succeffors.
And that the Country or Territory thus by
Us granted and defcrib'd, may be dignify'd
by Us with as large Titles and Privileges as
any other of Our Dominions and Territories in that Region,

Know ye, That We of Our further Grace,
certain Knowledge, and mere Motion, have
thought fit to erect the fame Tract of
Ground, Country and Ifland, into a Province,
and out of the Fulnefs of our Royal Power
ane Prerogative, We do for Us, Our Heirs
and Succeffors, erect and incorporate the
fame into a Province, and do name it *Carolana*, or the Province of *Carolana*, and the
faid Iflands the *Carolana* Iflands, and fo from
henceforth will have them call'd, *&c.*

In Witnefs, &c.

Witnefs the King at Weftminfter *the Thir-
tieth Day of* October, *in the Fifth Year of
Our Reign.*

NB. There are divers other Grants,
Licences and Privileges, Royalties, and Immunities, in the faid *Charter* contain'd and fet
forth, which, upon perufal thereof will
more fully and at large appear.

The Additional Claufe from the Board
of Trade.

To

To the King's most Excellent MAJESTY,

May it please Your MAJESTY,

IN Obedience to Your MAJESTY's Commands signified to us by the Right Honourable Mr. *Secretary Vernon*, upon the Petition of Dr. *Coxe* in Relation to the Province of *Carolana*, alias *Carolana Florida*, We have consider'd his said Petition, and humbly crave leave to represent unto Your MAJESTY.

THAT Your MAJESTY's Attorney-General upon the Perusal of Letters Patents and Conveyances produc'd to him by Dr. *Coxe*, has reported to us his Opinion, That Dr. *Coxe* has a good Title in Law to the said Province of *Carolana*, extending from 31 to 36 Degrees of *North* Latitude inclusive, on the Continent of *America*, and to several adjacent Islands.

Sign'd

Whitehall,
Dec. 21. 1699.

Stamford
Lexington
P. Meadows
William Blathwait.
John Pollexfen
Abraham Hill
George Stepney

I

An

An Abstract of the first Memorial presented to King William, *being a Demonstration of the just Pretensions of his* MAJESTY *the King of* England *unto the Province of* Carolana, *alias* Florida, *and of the present Proprietor under his* MAJESTY.

SEBASTION *Cabota* in the Year 1497, by the Commission and at the Expence of King *Henry* VII. discover'd all the Coast of *America*, fronting the *North* or *Atlantick* Ocean, from the Degrees of 56 to 28 of *North* Latitude, Twenty Years before any other *Europeans* had visited that vast Continent; As appears not only from our own Historians and Cosmographers, but also from the Testimony of the most eminent amongst the *Spanish*, viz. *Peter Martyr* their great Secretary in his *Decades*; *Oviedo* Governor of *Hispaniola*; *Herrera* their celebrated Historian, and *Gomara*, unto whom We appeal: As also unto the famous *Ramusio*, a most impartial Person, Secretary to the renowned Republick of *Venice*, whose Works were Printed in the Year 1550; and his elegant Contemporary *Paulus Jovius*.

ABOUT Twenty Years after, the *Southern* Part of this Continent adjacent to the Gulph of *Bahama*, and that afterwards styl'd the Gulph of *Mexico*, was visited first by the *Spaniards* commanded by *Juan Ponce de Leon*. Ten Years after, *Vasquez Ayllon* landed upon it, with a more considerable Force; and
in

in the Year 1527 *Pamphilo Narvaez* with a greater : Next to him in the Year 1539. *Ferdinando Soto.* But their enormous Cruelties did so enrage the Natives, that they successively expell'd them. And these pretended Conquerors, cannot have a much worse Character, bestow'd upon them by their Enemies or Foreigners, than they receive from their own Historians, and that so ill as almost exceeds Credit.

THE last Expedition of the *Spaniards*, unto that Part of *Florida*, now *Carolana*, which borders upon the Gulph of *Mexico*, was in the Year 1558, by the Orders of *Don Luys de Velasco*, then Vice-Roy of *Mexico*; but the *Spaniards* after their Arrival falling into great Feuds, return'd without making any Settlement. Nor have they ever since made upon this vast Continent, except that of St. *Augustine*, situated upon the *North* Sea, between the 29th and 30th Degrees of *Northern* Latitude, above 1200 Miles distant from *Panuco*, their nearest Habitation to the *West*, which is 60 Leagues from *Mexico*. * The *French* indeed attempted a Settlement about Fourteen Years since at a Place they nam'd St. *Louis* Bay, not far from *Panuco* between 26 and 27 Degrees *North* Latitude, but were soon dispers'd. † And again this Year under Monsieur *Iberville*, and built a Sconce near the *West* and least Branch of *Meschacebe*, leaving therein about 40 Men.

I 2   KING

* *Vide* p. 38, and 39. † *Vid.* p. 81.

KING *Charles* I. in the Fifth Year of his
Reign, granted unto Sir *Robert Heath* his
Attorney-General, a Patent of all that Part
of *America*, from the River St. *Mattheo*, lying and being in 30 Degrees of *North* Latitude, unto the River *Paſſo Magno* in 36
Degrees; extending in Longitude from the
North or *Atlantick* Ocean, unto the *Pacifick*
or *South*-Sea, not then being in the actual
Poſſeſſion of any Chriſtian Prince or State.
And no Part of this Grant was then or
ſince in the actual Poſſeſſion of any Chriſtian Prince or State, excepting St. *Auguſtine*
aforeſaid; and. *New Mexico*, a great Province, unto which the *Engliſh* lay no Claim.

SIR *Robert Heath* in the Thirteenth Year
of King *Charles* I. convey'd the Premiſes
unto the Lord *Mattravers*, ſoon after, upon
his Father's Deceaſe, Earl of *Arundel* and
Surrey, Earl Marſhal of *England*, who at
great Expence planted ſeveral Parts of the
ſaid Country, and had effected much more,
had he not been prevented by the War
with *Scotland*, in which he was General for
King *Charles*; and afterwards by the Civil
Wars in *England*, and the Lunacy of his
Eldeſt Son.

IN the Beginning of the Protectorate of
Cromwel, One Captain *Watts* (afterwards
knighted by King *Charles* II. and by him
made Governor of St. *Chriſtophers*) falling
accidentally upon the Coaſt of *Florida*, and
meeting with One *Leet* an *Engliſhman*, who
having

having divers Years before been ſhipwreck'd,
and the only Man eſcap'd, and then in great
Favour with the chief *Paraſouſſi* or Roytelet
of that Country, by his Influence the *Engliſh* were permitted to trade, and kindly
invited to ſettle there. Not long after the
King as they ſtyl'd him, ſent One of his
chief Subjects Embaſſador to *England* ; and
the *Engliſh* had divers Tracts of Land given
them by the *Indians*, and ſurvey'd that
Continent (a Map whereof is ſtill in being)
for above Two Hundred Miles ſquare.

AFTER this a great Number of Perſons
engag'd to contribute conſiderably, towards
the ſettling a Colony of *Engliſh* in the ſaid
Province, which Original Subſcription is
now in my Poſſeſſion. They nam'd divers
Places, eſpecially Rivers, Harbors and Iſles,
by the Names of the Captains of Ships,
chief Traders, and other Circumſtances relating to the *Engliſh* Nation, as by the ſaid
Map or Chart doth more fully appear.

IN the Year 1678, a conſiderable Number of Perſons went from *New England* upon Diſcovery, and proceeded ſo far as *New
Mexico*, 150 Leagues beyond the River
Meſchacebe, and at their Return render'd an
Account to the Government of *Boſton*, as
will be atteſted, among many others, by
Colonel *Dudley*, then One of the Magi-
ſtrates, afterwards Governor of *New England*, and at preſent Deputy Governor of
the Iſle of *Wight*, under the Honourable
the

the Lord *Cutts*. The War soon after break-
ing out between the *English* and *Indians*,
many of the *Indians*, who were in that
Expedition, retreated to *Canada*, from whom
Monsieur *De Salle* receiv'd most of his Information, concerning that Country, by
him afterwards more fully discover'd. And
they serv'd him for Guides and Interpre-
ters ; as is attested by Monsieur *Le Tonty*,
who accompany'd Monsieur *De Salle* : As
also by Monsieur *Le Clerk*, in a Book publish'd by Order of the *French* King. For
which Reason, and divers other Passages
favouring inadvertently the *English* Pretensions, his Journal Printed at *Paris*, was called in, and that Book of One Livre Price,
is not now to be purchas'd for Thirty
Livres.

The Five Nations, in the Territory of
New York, commonly call'd *Irocois* by the
French, who have for above Thirty Years
voluntarily subjected themselves to the King
of *England*, had conquer'd all that Part of
the Country, from their own Habitations
to and beyond *Meschacebe* (as the aforemention'd Monsieur *Le Tonty* more than once
acknowledges : As also Father *Le Clerk* in
his History of *Canada* Printed by Order in
1691) sold, made over and surrender'd,
all their Conquests and Acquisitions therein,
to the Government of *New York*, which
therefore of Right belongs to the *English*.

THE

THE Prefent Proprietary of *Carolana* apprehending, from what Information he had receiv'd, that the Planting of this Country would be highly beneficial to the *Englifh*, endeavour'd divers Ways to acquaint himfelf with the People, Soil and Products thereof; difcover'd divers of its Parts; firft from *Carolina*, afterwards from *Penfilvania*, by the *Sufquehanah* River; and many of his People travell'd to *New Mexico*.

SOON after the faid Proprietary of *Carolana*, made another Difcovery more Southerly, by the great River *Uchequiton*, and receiv'd an Account of that Country before altogether unknown, and whereunto the *French* to this Day are utter Strangers.

THE faid Proprietary, about the fame Time, made another Difcovery more to the North-Weft, beyond the River *Mefchacebe*, of a very great Sea or Lake of frefh Water, feveral Thoufand Miles in Circumference; and of a great River, at the S. W. End, iffuing out into the *South-Sea*, about the Latitude of 44 Degrees; which was then communicated to the Privy-Council, and a Draft thereof left in the Plantation Office.

AND fince We are affur'd, the *Englifh* have more fully difcover'd the faid Lake from the *South-Sea*, and enter'd by Shipping thereinto.

THEY likewife coafted all that great Continent unto the Seas of *Tartary* and *Japan*,

pan, found it going and returning a very easy quick and safe Navigation, and the People much civiliz'd; and during the Voyage, though they did not (in the Places where they call'd) stay in the whole Ten Days, yet they obtain'd, by Barter with the Natives, above Fourscore Pound Weight of pure Gold.

DIVERS other Parts of this Country were discover'd by the *English*, from several Colonies, long before the *French* had the least Knowledge thereof. Colonel *Wood* in *Virginia* inhabiting at the Falls of *James* River, above 100 Miles West of *Chesepeack* Bay, from the Year 1654 to 1664, discover'd at several Times, several Branches of the great Rivers *Ohio* and *Meschacebe*. I was possess'd about Twenty Years ago of the Journal of Mr. *Needham* employ'd by the aforesaid Colonel, and it is now in the Hands of, *&c.*

THE *English* have not only survey'd by Land the greatest Part of *Florida* and *Carolana*, but have been as industrious and successful in their Attempts by Sea. The present Proprietary of *Carolana*, 23 Years ago, was possess'd of a Journal from the Mouth of the *Meschacebe*, where it disembogues itself into the *Mexican* Gulph, unto the Yellow or Muddy River, as they call it; which said Journal was in *English*, and seem'd to have been written many Years before; together with a very large Map or Chart,

with

with the Names of divers Nations, and
short Hints of the chief Products of each
Country. And by Modern Journals of *English* and *French*, the most material Parts
thereof are confirm'd, the Nations, in divers
Places there nam'd, continuing still in the
same Stations, or very little remote. From
a Confidence in these Journals, the *English*
were encourag'd to attempt further Discoveries by Sea and Land. And the present
Proprietary hath expended therein, for his
Share only, above Nine Thousand Pounds,
as he can easily and readily demonstrate.

THE last Year being 1698, the present
Proprietary, at his own Expence, set out
Two Ships from *England* well Mann'd and
Victuall'd; order'd a *Barcolongo* to be bought
at *Carolina*, purposely built for that Coast,
and for Discovery of Shoals, Lagunes or
Bays, and Rivers; As also all Materials
for building and equipping another Ship in
the Country. One of these Ships returning,
was unhappily cast away upon the *English*
Coast in a great Storm, but very providen-
tially the Journal was sav'd, though all the
Men were lost; which Journal contains an
ample Account of the Country all along the
Coast, which they represent as the most pleasant in the World, and abounding with all
Things, not only for Necessity, but for the
Comfort of Human Life. And amongst many
others, there's a Draft of one of the most Ca-
pacious Harbors in the Universe, the most in-

K   viting

viting Place imaginable for building a
Town and establishing a Colony, the Adjacent Country being pleasant, fruitful, and
a very great Tract of Land freed from
Trees ready for Planting ; an excellent
Quarry of Stone like that of *Portland*, and
a great Oyster Bank almost touching the
very Quarry, which will supply them with
Lime, for many Ages ; besides many other
Encouragements , which are comprehended
in another Memorial.

D. COXE.

F I N I S.

ERRATA.

PAGE 2. L. 17. read, *where.* p. 4. l. 28. r. *Carolana,* p. 9 l. 10. r.
their. p. 10. l. 3. r. *their.* p. 11. last Lale. r. *Cheroaners.* p. 12. l. 16.
dele *Hohio.* p. 15. l. 18. r. *Ozages.* p. 16. l. 16. r. *Paneassa's.* p. 17. l. 19.
r. *Illinoeeck.* l. 21. r. *Caracakianos.* l. ult. r. *the.* p. 23. l. 16. r. *Palachena.*
l. 11. r. *Guaxula.* p. 36. l. 6. r. *enter.* p. 42. l. 13. r. *all most.* p. 45. l.
33. r. *this.* p. 56. l. 11. r. *Onroiens* or *Oiongonens.* p. 61 l. 29. r. *Carolana.*
p. 63. l. 31. dele *especially* America. l. 32. dele *nrither,* dele *New.* l. 33.
dele, *and, add, to.* p. 67. l. 24. r. *Hilum.* l. 33. r. *Nortzinskoy.* p. 76. l. 32.
between *they* and *make,* add *may.* p. 83. l. 4. for *Florida,* r. *Mexico.* p. 88.
l. 10. and 11. r. *Oronoque.* Besides some Errors in the Pointing, which
the observing Reader may correct with his Pen.

INDEXES.

INDEX TO *CAROLANA*.

(Page i is the beginning of the preface.)

Barba, Alonso, 98
Batavia, 66
Bay, Hudson's, xxvii, 4, 21, 43; Spirito Santo, 7, 26, 29, 33; Chesepeack (Chesepeak), 13, 54, 120; Palache, 22; Nassau, 25, 29; Bilocchy, 30; Fresh-Water, 34; Salt-Water, 34–35; St. Bernard, 38; St. Louis, 38, 115; Sakinam, 46; Poutouotamis, 47; Bear, 48
Beads, 82
Bears, 79
Beavour (beaver), 46–47, 49, 60, 79–80
Bebello, 107
Bengale, 91
Bilocohi, 31
Bitumen, 86–87
Blathwait [Blathwayt], William, 113
Blefkins, 66
Bond, [William] Captain, Mississippi, Expedition of 1698–1700, ii, iv
Boston, 117
Brandy, 51, 75
Brasil (Brazil), 87, 97, 104–105
Bread, 72, 74; Cassavi, 72
Breton, Cape, xiii, xxviii, xxix
Buffaloes, 37, 79
Bullion, xliv, 98
Byana, 86

Cabota, Sebastion, 114
Caesar, xx
Caffine, 96
California Peninsula, 64
Cammels (camels), 79, 89
Campeche, 29, 94
Canada, viii, x, xxi–xxii, xxvii–xxviii, xxix, 18, 26, 45–46, 59–60, 118; *History of*, 118
Cantons, 57, 61
Capers, 81
Carniola, 101
Carolana, i, iv, xxii, xxiv, xxvii, xxxviii, xlvii, L, 1–2, 72, 102, 112–115, 119–120
Carolina, xiv, xxxvii, L, 1–4, 13–14, 22, 48, 61, 73, 81, 119, 121
Carthaginians, 106
Carts, 77–78, 87
Caspian Sea, 89
Castrilome, 66
Cattle, 51, 71, 77–78
Charcoal, 93

Indexes.

INDEX TO THE INTRODUCTION.